The Complete
CHOCOLATE CHIP
COOKIE BOOK

The Complete CHOCOLATE CHIP COOKIE BOOK

by BOB & SUZANNE STAT
ILLUSTRATED BY RICHARD ANDERSON

A Dell/Banbury Book

Published by
Banbury Books, Inc.
37 West Avenue
Wayne, Pennsylvania 19087

Dell ® TM 681510, Dell Publishing Co., Inc.
ISBN: 0-440-01273-2
Printed in the United States of America
First printing — December 1982

3 teaspoons	= 1 tablespoon
2 tablespoons	= ⅛ cup
4 tablespoons	= ¼ cup
16 tablespoons	= 1 cup
16 ounces	= 1 pound
Dash	= a few drops
8 ounces	= 1 cup
1 cup	= ½ pint
2 cups	= 1 pint
2 pints	= 1 quart

BUTTER OR MARGARINE

1 pound (4 sticks)	= 2 cups
1 stick	= ½ cup (4 ounces)
½ stick	= 4 tablespoons

FLOUR

1 pound	= 2 cups

SUGAR

1 pound granulated	= 2 cups
1 pound confectioners'	= 3¾ cups
1 pound brown	= about 2¾ cups

An Introduction

A S WE ALL KNOW, the chocolate chip cookie is more than a food. It is an institution with a hallowed history and time-honored traditions. It is an industry, burgeoning with innovation and entrepreneurs. It is an almost purely American phenomenon with an international reputation. Which is to say, the chocolate chip cookie is the big time.

But deep in the hearts of those who love the crunch and goo of a freshly baked wafer loaded with chunks of semi-sweet chocolate, there is the sure and simple knowledge that all the hoopla surrounding chocolate chip cookies misses the point. In fact, articles in *Time* magazine and *The Wall Street Journal* concerning our favorite edible somehow malign the essence of the things. Somehow cheapen their no-frills, homey wonderfulness. For the perfect chocolate chip cookie was made, long ago and far away, in a kitchen you fondly recall as having had funny-looking linoleum and a table with chrome legs. If you try

you can probably remember the dog drooling in the corner and the sound of the screen door slapping as your little brother made off with a fistful of bits.

There's no way around it. Try as you might, you cannot separate your love of the chocolate chip cookie from an idealized, sentimentalized reminiscence of some cookie in your past. Which is why the chocolate chip cookie is the perfect food for our troubled times.

In an age grown accustomed to thinking the unthinkable, in a world laden with conflict, economic turmoil and general nastiness, the chocolate chip cookie comes to the rescue. And it does so with simple eloquence, posing the question, "How can the perfect cookie, so dimly remembered, be re-created in my own kitchen?"

Now this query at first may seem insignificant in light of weightier matters. To a few tasteless and presumptuous souls it even may seem trivial and distracting. But actually, the issue is crucial precisely because it is so profoundly innocent, so completely and simultaneously important and unimportant.

Which is the guiding principle behind this book. Herein you will find no overblown concern for precision, no tedious descriptions of detailed techniques, no solemn worries or picayune cautions. Instead, this book will show you just how much fun the quest for the perfect chocolate chip cookie can be. And in so doing, it will demonstrate that these edibles are hearty and

reliable, essentially impossible to louse up.

Which brings us back to the purpose of the chocolate chip cookie in the modern world. It seems to me that the best thing about these cookies is their stout New England heritage and reputation for trustworthiness. You can count on a chocolate chip cookie. Rely on it. As long as you follow a few simple instructions, you can be absolutely certain that you'll bake something terrific. And it is for this reason that the authors would like to prescribe chocolate chip cookie-making as the perfect therapy in an altogether unreliable world. Baking your own will make you feel better.

The perfect chocolate chip cookie is not so crispy as
to be dry, nor so gooey as to be wet.

A Sort of History

THERE IS SOMETHING wonderfully appropriate about the origins of the chocolate chip cookie. Something instructive, in an odd sort of way. For the tale has a nifty quirk in it that gets right to the heart of this remarkable food's true nature. And like so many oft-told tales, this story seems to be endowed with a special quality, as though some mischievous culinary muse with a warped sense of humor has hidden a chuckle-to-live-by in this bit of kitchen history. The trick, of course, is to find the punch line in the parable.

The tale begins in 1930, an unhappy year for business start-ups. Still, for reasons that remain mysterious, Ruth and Kenneth Wakefield decided then to buy an old house halfway between Boston and New Bedford, Massachusetts. In years past the building had served as an inn and changing station, a place where travelers could switch horses while plodding down Route 18. The Wakefields renovated the house and

turned it into a restaurant with rooms for rent on the second floor. It was then dubbed the Toll House.

Now, Mrs. Wakefield was an enterprising woman and a good cook as well. So it wasn't long before her kitchen was a reasonably busy place, serving meals to a healthy number of customers. And, feeling passably expert, she decided one day to experiment with a popular recipe of the time, one for a simple cookie known as the Butter Drop-Do. This cookie, a straightforward, yellowish thing made from flour, butter, sugar, eggs and vanilla is light, sweet and tasty. Just for the record, here's the recipe:

> 1 *cup plus 2 tablespoons sifted all-purpose flour*
> ½ *teaspoon salt*
> ½ *teaspoon baking soda*
> ½ *cup butter, softened*
> 6 *tablespoons brown sugar*
> 6 *tablespoons granulated sugar*
> 1 *egg*
> ½ *teaspoon vanilla extract*

Oven temperature: 375°F

In a large mixing bowl, sift flour, salt and baking soda. In a separate bowl, cream both kinds of sugar with butter until mixture is creamy. Add egg and vanilla to mixture and blend well. Stir in flour mixture and blend until no trace of flour is visible. Drop from teaspoon onto greased cookie sheets, leaving enough room for cookies to spread. Bake 8-10 minutes. Makes 4 dozen cookies.

Clearly, there's nothing very fancy about a Butter Drop-Do, least of all its name. But it's a yeomanlike treat, almost impossible to ruin and always good to eat. Considering this, Mrs. Wakefield decided to spruce up the cookie. So she chopped a semi-sweet chocolate bar into little hunks and mixed it into her batter. It seems she thought that the chocolate would melt, spreading itself through her finished cookies, turning them into something like Chocolate Butter Drop-Do cookies. Obviously, good old Ruth Wakefield was wrong. For the simple fact of the matter is that cookies cook faster than chocolate melts. And, rather than burn her experiment, she took her botched effort out of the oven and let it cool.

It isn't difficult to imagine this unlikely pioneer's surprise when she sampled the odd-looking wafers she'd created. Of course, they were terrific.

As certainly as the creation of the wheel, the discovery of penicillin and the development of the theory of relativity were bound to gain widespread acceptance, so too Ruth Wakefield's cookies became very popular. Diners in her restaurant bought tons of them. And they requested her recipe. Folks baked them at home, gave them to friends, talked them up all over the place. Thus did the word go forth: mix chopped chocolate into Butter Drop-Do batter and you've got something really worth eating.

Within months the better part of Massachusetts was flailing away at chocolate bars, making cookies. But to do so they had to buy the chocolate and so sales of this essential ingredient soared

in the area immediately surrounding Ruth's establishment. Nestlé, an alert organization that recognized the disproportionate sales growth in the region as a good thing, sent a representative to the Wakefields' restaurant to inquire about Ruth's invention.

Not long thereafter the company began marketing chocolate bars that were scored and packed with a little cutting tool for making chocolate chunks. Cookie lovers thought this was a good idea ...and bought loads of

them. So many, in fact, that in 1939 Nestlé packaged the first chocolate bits and printed Ruth's recipe on the back of that famous yellow bag.

Mrs. Wakefield, by now quite well-known, published a book, *The Toll House Cook Book*. The sublime recipe in it differs slightly from the one on the back of the Nestlé package of bits, but not much. So you know, she called her cookies "Toll House Chocolate Crunch Cookies."

The rest, as they say, is history. Consider, if you will, the following: Over 240 million chocolate morsels are purchased *every day* in the United States. Chocolate industry statisticians figure that Americans bake over 7 billion chocolate chip cookies a year. And the U.S. Department of Agriculture estimates that about 8 billion dollars' worth of the cookies are sold annually. Needless to say, the chocolate chip cookie business is colossal.

But the point, I think, is not that Ruth Wakefield developed a superb concoction, perfect in its design, flawlessly conceived, unsurpassed and unsurpassable. Instead, she bungled onto a good thing. She goofed, brilliantly. And then she was smart enough to recognize her serendipity and make the most of it. Which, in a way, roughly describes the essence of all chocolate chip cookies. They are combinations of any number of peculiar ingredients added to an

The U.S.D.A. reports . . .

altogether delightful, inevitably delicious basic cookie. That is, the things are so good, so naturally scrumptious, so easy to bake correctly, so quintessentially delectable and constantly magnificent that it's virtually impossible to ruin them.

Moral: If a chocolate chip cookie is nothing more than a Butter Drop-Do gone wrong, then the world is a wonderful place indeed.

People

SOMEWHERE in the back of every true chocolate chip cookie lover's mind is the clear and certain knowledge that his mother made the very best cookies. Absolutely. No question about it. None even come close. And, just as surely, we all know that the second best cookies on earth are made by a neighbor or an aunt or a sister with a rambling country kitchen and a light snow falling. Some magic in the alchemy of combining the simple ingredients in a chocolate chip cookie makes such truths universally accepted and hardly ever discussed.

Still there are those misguided souls who continually attempt to convince the American public that their efforts are superior to all others. This is probably the case because they not only make good cookies but also sell them. And it's hard to sell something if you are openly willing to admit it isn't really the best. As a result, the last few years have produced an astounding array of cookie purveyors who sell a mind-boggling number of chocolate chip cookies. Every one of which is the very best.

What's more, since the chocolate chip cookie business is a growth industry (similar to cable television and micro-computers), there is a certain redundancy to the naming of the companies that sell them. Consider, for instance, The Cookie Connection,

An aunt, baking.

The Cookie Works, The Cookie Factory, The Cookie Store, We Got Your Cookie, Kiss My Cookies, Springwater Cookies, Cookies Cook'n, Zaro's Cookie Corner, Mrs. Field's Chocolate Chippery, Rippety Chippety, The Chipyard and, immodestly, The Original Great American Chocolate Chip Cookie Company.

Among the many who make and sell chocolate chip cookies there are, however, a few legendary people you should know about. The best-known of them, it seems, is Wally "Famous" Amos. This ebullient gentleman struggled through a variety of jobs until, one day, he found himself an agent in the entertainment business. Happily for the rest of us, he wasn't particularly successful at it. But he understood the vital concept of self-promotion and so began baking his Aunt Della's recipe for chocolate chip cookies. As he made his rounds, dutifully trying to aid the careers of entertainers such as Abby Lincoln and Franklin Ajaye, he gave cookies away as a kind of calling card.

It wasn't long before he (and a great many others) noticed that Wally Amos and his cookies had heftier reputations than the folks he represented. Following the axiom "Do what you do best," he opened a cookie store. Today, the Famous Amos Chocolate Chip Cookie is handmade in both New Jersey and California, and sells in thousands of department stores, specialty shops, supermarkets and gourmet salons. And for good reason. Famous Amos makes a very, very good cookie. 7,000 pounds of them a day.

David Liederman is another altogether notable cookie baker. A chef trained by the Troisgros brothers in Roanne, France, David sells five varieties of chocolate chip cookies out of his shops in New England, Illinois, Tennessee and other places. His retail outlets bake right on the premises using Land O Lakes butter, Lindt bittersweet chocolate (hand-chopped into a variety of sizes and shapes), high butterfat milk and Hecker's un-bleached flour.

David's Cookie Kitchens produce a slightly oversized, definitely pliant, arguably squashy, outrageously popular bunch of delicacies that sell like crazy even at $5.00 a pound. To be honest, no true connoisseur of the gooey and still-warm should fail to stop at David's if given the opportunity.

But David's culinary abilities aren't the best thing about him. He is the proud owner of a framed, notarized letter from his mother attesting to the fact that his first word was "cookie."

There are many other rather remarkable cookie people. Richard La Motta, for instance, invented the Chipwich, 3½ ounces of ice cream between two chocolate chip cookies. And Marolyn Schwartz makes 13 inches in diameter giants for business meetings, each of which contains a pound of morsels. Dale Robinette markets cookies in the shape of and mimicking the packaging of Dog Bones. He calls them People Bones.

An industrial cookie spy.

People sell cookies from pushcarts, trucks, storefronts, their back doors and out of the trunks of cars. And, in the spirit of all-American good fun, industrial spies steal recipes and manufacturers guard their trade secrets as though they had near-nuclear significance.

It is, of course, unfair to suggest that somehow the chocolate chip cookie ought to escape the competitive world of free enterprise. It's silly to imagine that anything so desperately adored by so many could be limited to amateur kitchens. For we all know that, when the wondrously un-deserved bounty of *three* of the *really* best chocolate chip cookies on earth found their way into our lunch bags at school, each and every one of us promptly ate two and then tried to trade the third for a Ted Williams baseball card or a matching pair of Barbie Doll shoes. It's the American way.

Worries

BY ITS VERY NATURE, this book must assume the role of advocate in any debate regarding chocolate chip cookies. After all, this is more than a cookbook, it's a statement of faith, a homage to and glorification of the world's most spectacular snack. However, it should not be assumed that the authors are blindly loyal to these near-perfect edibles. In spite of having devoted the better part of our adult lives to collecting recipes, baking variations and testing ingredients for the sole purpose of making better cookies, we remain objective. And so, before discarding with extreme ridicule any complaint or criticism of the chocolate chip cookie, we briefly consider the logic (hah!) and evidence (always circumstantial) that seek to malign our defenseless favorite.

For instance, a brief look at any chocolate chip cookie recipe immediately will yield the makings of a good argument. There is a reasonably substantial amount of sugar in the things. And, were one concerned about weight gain, this might prove troubling. But it is myopic to conclude, out of hand, that chocolate chip cookies are fattening, per se. Such reasoning simply doesn't consider all the facts.

Extensive research reveals that the average homemade chocolate chip cookie contains 142 calories. Mixing cookie batter, on the other hand, consumes about 325 calories per hour. And jogging in place burns up fully 550 calories per hour.

Based on this information several conclusions can be drawn. First, if one mixes and bakes chocolate chip cookies slowly enough and in small enough batches, eating the goodies as you do so, the effort of making the cookies will consume *all* the calories taken in by your body. Of course, you must prepare each cookie individually, jogging in place while it bakes, but the system works.

More important, should you bake 144 cookies to a batch and eat them over a two-day period while relaxing, you will have consumed enough net calories to discover a cure for cancer or negotiate world peace. Considered in this light it is clearly impossible to criticize the caloric content of chocolate chip cookies.

Having disposed of the trivial concern involving

Jog while you bake.

calories, one must address the question of tooth decay. After all, both chocolate and sugar are notoriously bad for kids' teeth. But, no less reputable an institution than M.I.T. (in a study sponsored by the Chocolate Manufacturers Association) found that chocolate apparently contains some sort of protein that actually *inhibits* bacterial growth on the teeth. The report did not go so far as to suggest that we all brush daily with Nestlé's morsels, but clearly, the bits aren't all that bad for you. And to further defend this position, the Eastman Dental Center in Rochester, New York, discovered that chocolate chip cookies are among the snacks that least promote tooth decay. So there.

And as if all that weren't enough, in a not altogether breezy but decidedly comprehensive report in the *Annals of Allergy* (yes, they have a magazine for allergies), one Dr. Joseph Fries reported that chocolate is not universally responsible for acne. Huzzah.

Critics of chocolate chip cookies, when presented with the irrefutable evidence offered here, invariably resort to what is known in debating circles as the cheap shot. They claim that chocolate chip cookies are obviously habit forming and potentially addictive. Now we all know that the sugar in cookies offers the body a quick and reliable surge of energy. And it is common knowledge that this energy produces a sense of well-being. Moreover, it is true that people tend to do things that make them feel good over and over again. But it is irresponsible to infer from this that cookies are habit forming. It's clearly not the cookies but rather the feeling good that is habit forming. And, when compared to fingernail biting and cigarette smoking, feeling good isn't such a bad habit.

The last and most insidious slur that is directed toward chocolate chip cookies involves the chips themselves. Scientists have actually isolated a chemical, phenylethylamine, in chocolate that is an amphetaminelike substance almost identical to the one produced naturally in the brain of a person in love. In this regard, chocolate can be defended by a simple, parallel observation. Scientists also have discovered that rigorous jogging causes the body to manufacture a chemical very much like opium. But nobody criticizes joggers. They pick on people in love with chocolate chip cookies.

It also should be pointed out that a dozen chocolate chip cookies contain more protein than an ounce of Swiss cheese, more calcium than a tablespoon of milk, more iron than a steak, and perfectly respectable amounts of vitamin A, thiamine, riboflavin, niacin and potassium. Pretty terrific, huh?

Tools

FOR MANY PEOPLE, baking chocolate chip cookies is like wearing tight shoes: it's not much fun but is worth doing because it feels so good when you're finished and get to the real point of the endeavor, in this case, eating. And, to be honest, if I could buy a cookie as good as those that come fresh and hot from my oven, I probably would do so, thus saving myself the chore of vacuuming spilled flour from the kitchen floor. But, since truly great cookies require a certain rite of passage (called mixing) and the patience of Job (waiting the ten or so interminable minutes for the first batch to bake), it seems only sensible to enjoy yourself while you're at it. In order to do so you need plenty of time and the right tools.

Not many are required. And they don't have to be expensive. But you need them all and they might as well be solid, workable, comfortable to be around and do their jobs admirably. Utensils of this kind make the great fun and hard work of cooking much more pleasant. As they say, a good workman doesn't blame his tools primarily because he owns the very best.

A Bowl.

Most imaginations would have it that chocolate chip cookie batter ought to be mixed in a great, thick-lipped, glossy ceramic bowl. The sort you can embrace. The kind that has huge stripes painted on its side and a small chip in it somewhere. A bowl that has already seen a thousand batches of cookies come and go. A bowl so big it is stored high in the cupboard because it's only used for mixing baked goods. Such a container needs, of course, a smooth, stained, long-handled wooden spoon to go with it. A strong and ancient utensil capable of plowing through even the stiffest batter. But, while this imagined wonder will certainly do the job, it isn't really the ideal bowl. Instead, the best of them accompany an electric mixer. Such bowls are often stainless steel, shiny, efficient and not very lovable. In fact, mixers usually come with two bowls, the larger of which (of course) you'll use in making your batter.

Measuring Cups.

There are two varieties of measuring cups. The best known are glass or plastic, and have markings on their sides to indicate various volumes in the cup. This type is used to measure liquids. Never, ever dry ingredients. You probably should have a 2-cup measuring cup of this kind.

But you'll also need a set of measuring cups for dry ingredients. These are usually metal, a kind of worn-looking grey with a simple, flat handle. Each, when filled to overflowing and then leveled with a spatula or knife, contains exactly the amount of ingredient called for. Normally, a set of these includes ¼, ⅓, ½ and 1-cup cups. If you make cookies in large batches or often or both, you might like to find a 2-cup cup as many recipes call for this amount of flour.

It is important, when measuring dry ingredients, to dole out precise amounts of whatever is called for. In the case of chips, however, certain liberties are allowed.

Measuring Spoons. Unlike measuring cups, the spoons do double duty. That is, they parcel out prescribed amounts of both liquids and dry ingredients. A standard set of them, including ⅛ teaspoon, ¼ teaspoon, ½ teaspoon, 1 teaspoon and 1 tablespoon, is required to make cookies. Remember, too, that when measuring dry stuff like salt or baking soda, you treat spoons the same way you handle measuring cups. That is, you fill the spoon to overflowing and then level the contents by scraping off the excess. Which is to say that a ½ teaspoon of baking soda is a *leveled* ½ teaspoon of baking soda.

One other thought. There is no denying the economy and durability of plastic cooking utensils. These modern conveniences don't break or bend or dent. If you drop them they don't shatter. And nearly all are made so that they don't melt in a dishwasher. Still, for purely arbitrary, definitely sentimental reasons, this text has a profound bias against plastic. It's, ya know, so *plastic*. However, in the case of measuring spoons there is an excellent argument for selecting the bright, colorful sort rather than the time-honored metal spoons. It's simple: sooner or later you will be obliged to entertain an obstreperous, fretful, whining one-year-old child in your home. This creature may even be your own. When this inevitable event occurs, you can mollify the little monster (as I do my daughter) with your multi-colored, indestructible, plastic measuring spoons.

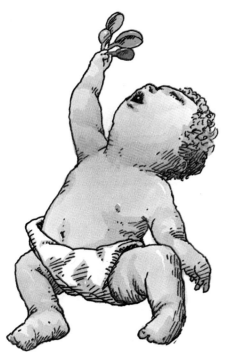

There's nothing like plastic to keep a kid happy.

Wax Paper. Incredibly, wax paper is a stranger to many members of the younger generation, born and raised in a world that wraps sandwiches in Baggies. Nevertheless, the chocolate chip cookie is destined to introduce such people to wax paper. There is simply no substitute for a sheet of it when you are sifting flour or straining brown sugar. Buy wide rolls so that cleaning the counter tops when you're finished is easier.

A Grater. Many cookie recipes call for grated lemon or orange rind. When you are preparing this ingredient, be sure to use the smallest, round holes on the grater and proceed with a delicate hand. You want small, fine bits, taken only from the very surface of the fruit. The lower, whiter layer of lemon or orange skin is something less than tasty.

Cookie Sheets.

The ideal cookie sheet, at least to my taste, is something of a contradiction. A traditionalist, I think that all cookie sheets should be old, suggesting somehow that they know what they're doing simply by having practiced so much. The trouble with old cookie sheets, though, is that they tend to become battered, dented or twisted. Whether this occurs through heating up and cooling down over and over again or whether all old cookie sheets have been used for sliding down a snow-covered hill remains a mystery. Regardless, old cookie sheets don't sit flat in an oven. They wobble. And so cookies made on them emerge misshapen or irregular.

Worse, old sheets tend to become quite discolored, especially on their undersides. As a result, they absorb heat faster than they should and can burn the bottom of a cookie before the top is properly cooked.

Thus, the best kind of cookie sheet is new and shiny, a bright, spotless, aluminum tray. And it has only one raised side, usually a short side. This design detail makes it easier either to lift cookies from the sheet or to slide an entire batch off with the aluminum foil under it. One other thing: a cookie sheet should be at least three inches smaller, all around, than the interior of your oven so that heat is free to circulate during the baking.

The ultimate fate of all cookie sheets depends on the average snowfall in their area.

An Electric Mixer.

It is possible and even fun to mix a batch of cookies by hand, stirring the batter with a spoon. There's something very satisfying about doing so. And when you're finished, you can take the spoon (or a finger) and scrape raw batter remnants from the bowl, snacking on what may be the world's most perfect food while your last batch of cookies bakes.

But if you confine yourself to this method, you'll not only have to work harder for your cookies, but you'll also miss the wonderful frustration of painstakingly licking batter from the interior of mixer beaters. This, of course, is an age-old ritual taught to children generation after generation. For this reason, you should use an electric mixer, even if it must be one of the portable, hand-held kinds.

Better yet, though, are those mixers that come on a hefty metal stand. These great, whirring appliances churn batter slowly, their bowls revolving patiently as two syncopated beaters mix away. This kind of mixer is best simply because it offers the hypnotic pleasure of watching batter spiral into the beaters as you spatula your mix off the sides of the bowl, forcing it to the center.

God bless beaters.

A Spatula.

A rubber-bladed spatula is better than a plastic one because the rubber bends, conforming to the shape of the side of any bowl.

A Sifter.

Flour is an extremely fine, white powder that comes in sacks. In your mixing bowl it should be light, soft, delicate, the airy basis of a great cookie. But in a sack it is dense, heavy, tightly confined and consequently packed down. Like newly fallen snow that a truck just drove over. If you measure one cup of unsifted flour into your batter, you are, in fact, adding close to a cup and two tablespoons or so. That is, unsifted flour is compacted. Even the kind that is sold as "presifted" flour should be sifted before being measured.

There are two sorts of sifters. One kind has a single, fine mesh. The other kind has three layers of screening through which the flour passes. If you have the simpler kind of sifter, you have to sift your flour twice before measuring it.

An Oven Thermometer.

The search, the quest, the ultimate goal of any profoundly committed chocolate chip cookie fanatic is to concoct the perfect cookie. Not merely excellent, more than terrific, definitely an epiphany of cookiedom. To do so

requires careful preparation, fresh and high-quality ingredients and, absolutely, the right oven temperature. Since no oven ever manufactured would satisfy a brain surgeon's sense of precision, there's no reason why you ought to trust yours. So, in order to be able to re-create your successes with predictable results, you need to preheat your oven to the proper temperature using an oven thermometer. By the way, mercury thermometers are the most accurate.

Never trust your oven.

Cooling Racks.

There are cooks in this world who, unbelievably, prepare chocolate chip cookies with exquisite care, bake them attentively and then cool their creations on paper towels. To do so borders on sacrilege. A hot chocolate chip cookie cooling on a dry, absorbent paper towel will give up precious quantities of essential oils, butter and dissolved spices. Worse, the things don't cool evenly because no air circulates under them. Thus, one must have cooling racks.

These aren't difficult to find. Most supermarkets sell them. But a proper chocolate chip cookie rack has at least one inch of air space under it. And racks that stand this tall can be difficult to locate. If you try but fail to locate them, prop your racks up using a cake pan or something similar.

Also, you need enough rack space to hold all the cookies on both your cookie sheets. When cookies come out of the oven, they should be removed from the sheets immediately so that they don't continue to cook.

A Strainer.   Brown sugar behaves like very ill-mannered flour. Given time and a little moisture, the sugar and molasses in brown sugar clumps into frustrating little nuggets that are impossible to do away with simply by mixing. And, since you don't want brown sugar surprises lodged inside your cookies, you have to break up these nuggets. The chore is easy enough. Using your fingertips, force the sugar through a strainer.

A Cookie Jar.

Chocolate chip cookies can be stored in a variety of ways and there's a short section in this book later on that describes several of them. However, some portion of any batch of cookies ought to be placed in a cookie jar. The sillier looking the better. Mine is a monstrous, grinning Humpty Dumpty half of whose head lifts off. It is important to put a few cookies in a jar as soon as they have cooled so that, two or three hours later when the aroma of the baking has left your kitchen, you can sneak to the jar, open its lid and inhale deeply.

Ingredients

BE HE A CABINET-MAKER, a gardener, an artist or a cook, anyone who works with his hands understands the importance of first-class raw materials. This is particularly true of the chocolate chip cookie chef. Not only do fresh, excellent ingredients improve the outcome of a cookie baker's efforts, they also make the process of mixing and baking more satisfying. More fun. And this sensitivity to ingredients that everyone who cooks develops goes well beyond the rational. For instance, implausible as it may sound, the delicate scent from a gently grated, very ripe, very fresh orange is far superior to that from a half-ripe, slightly shriveled fruit. The same is true of fresh, unsalted butter. Even though most recipes call for salt to be added to chocolate chip cookie batter, the things seem to taste better if you use unsalted butter. And eggs. Now, all things considered, there's almost no difference between a large and an extra-large egg when it comes to making cookie batter. But the extra-large ones have a better feel about them, as though you were lavishing some extravagance on your recipe.

Such considerations aren't really frivolous. To be sure, we all bake cookies to share with friends, offer up as gifts and to quiet relatives. They are used to impress our peers, entice loved ones and to ingratiate ourselves with those in a position to influence major events (like payday). But the ultimate arbiter, the final judge and most significant connoisseur of your cookies is you. And so, whether anyone else can taste the difference or not, *your* palate will discern the extra quality you've added to every ounce of batter.

One other, pertinent note. As has been strongly implied elsewhere in this slim volume, chocolate chip cookies are immensely popular with people for cooking in their own homes primarily because they are essentially unbotchable. Add to this comforting fact the knowledge that you have used good basic ingredients and you may well discover a world of confidence heretofore unimagined. Even as you mix your batter, you'll feel sure that your cookies are going to come out beautifully. That they can't be denied. That they're inevitable masterpieces. Surely, an attitude worth striving for.

Eggs.　It has been rumored that there are people who prefer some other food to chocolate chip cookies. While such an idea strains the normal, healthy imagination, it is possible, I suppose. Contemplating this fact, the authors conducted an extremely informal poll of about eleventy-seven not very randomly selected individuals and posed them the following question: "What food other than chocolate chip cookies can you honestly say brings elation to your soul and a smile to your lips?" Discarding all references to beverages (alcoholic and otherwise) and to chocolate (since, as we all know, chocolate is an ingredient, not a food), we tabulated the results. We thereby proved, absolutely, that all lovable foods contain eggs.

To a cook, there is nothing better than an egg. Eggs bring beauty to soufflés, body to cakes, richness to custards, a wonderful flavor to mayonnaise and hollandaise sauce and are great, hard-boiled, at a picnic. Eggs are not only terrific, they're versatile.

In selecting eggs there isn't much you have to worry about. Make sure they are as fresh as possible when you buy them. Don't concern yourself with the color of their shells or yolks. Neither factor has any influence whatever on your cookies. And, for baking, be sure to select either "large" or "extra-large" eggs.

There remains but one odd bit of advice regarding eggs. In almost all cooking the fresher the egg the better. If you've ever eaten a poached egg prepared from something plucked moments before from a hen's nest, you know how exceptionally good very fresh eggs are. They're really much better than those usually found in supermarkets. But, in baking of any kind, you should use eggs that are at least three days old. For some reason they form a better structure in your cookies and so rise better. Fortunately, almost all eggs available without an extra effort to procure very fresh eggs are at least two days old. So, buy them a day or two ahead of baking time.

Flour. In commercial greenhouses they have a saying, "He who controls the hose controls the profits." Meaning that regardless of the pesticides and fertilizers, the sun and air and work that go into growing plants, the outcome depends on whether you drown a plant, parch it or manage something in between. In the equally sensitive world of chocolate chip cookies, flour plays a similar role. It's the stuff that makes or breaks a cookie.

This fact acknowledged, you should know that all bags of flour are not created equal. All things considered, if you wander into a grocery store and choose a bag of flour, you're likely to have selected "all-purpose flour." This finely ground, white powder is a mixture of different kinds of wheats. Different wheats are mixed together in flour in order to vary the percentage of gluten in it. The ugliness of this stuff's name shouldn't upset you. It's gluten, found in greater quantities in hard wheats, that makes a flour become porous as it bakes. What's more, gluten acts a bit like glue in cookies, giving them the stick-together elasticity that bread has rather than the crumbliness of cake.

All-purpose flour is great in cookies. But you also should know that there's something called "cake flour" that you should avoid. This flour is made from very soft wheats and so has little gluten. It doesn't expand very much, doesn't form large pores and makes chocolate chip cookies that invariably fall apart as soon as you pick them up.

On the other hand, "bread flour" has loads of gluten in it. It yields cookies that are too tough.

It is interesting to note that a spectacular number of man-made disasters ranging from red dye to Love Canal have made most people fairly sensitive to what they eat. Unquestionably, this is good. However, the nutritional distinctions among bleached, unbleached and whole-grain flours is minuscule in a cookie. Especially when you consider that most people put a half-pound or so of pure butter in their batter. Put differently, the added protein in a whole-grain flour isn't going to offset the cholesterol in the butter.

But whole-grain flours do bring a different taste and texture to chocolate chip cookies and this is salient, to say the least. So, if you'd like to replace about half a recipe's demand for all-purpose flour with whole-grain flour, feel free. Simply be aware that there are often specks of wheat in these flours that won't go through a sifter. So having sifted, you have to shake the specks back into the flour and stir them in.

The chocolate chip cookie world, like almost all other fanatical but unofficial associations, contains its lunatic fringe. Members of this small but active group suffer from a wide variety of personality aberrations, not the least of which is uncontrolled tinkering. Which is very different, in degree if not kind, from healthy experimentation. The uncontrolled tinkerer substitutes something (occasionally anything) for everything in a chocolate chip cookie. And then adds all kinds of weird stuff. Like celery or (shudder) bubble gum.

This seems the appropriate point at which to report that a splinter group has formed at the very edge of the lunatic fringe. These people substitute various amounts of rice flour, rye flour, potato flour, tapioca flour, barley flour, cottonseed flour, peanut flour and oat flour for some of the good old-fashioned all-purpose flour in their cookie recipes. Amazing.

Not so bizarre, however, is the use of oatmeal in cookies. Its crunchy, absorbent nature lends grist to cookies. When you see it in a recipe, you are being asked to add *uncooked* oatmeal. Don't use instant kinds. And avoid those where the package calls for cooking any longer than five minutes.

Sugar.

A remarkable proportion of a chocolate chip cookie is made up of sugar. Which is to say that, by weight, it is a sugary cookie. Still, the things don't taste "sweet" as we normally understand the adjective. This is certainly because chocolate chip cookies employ a combination of tastes, a subtle blending of delectable ingredients, in order to produce their awesome appeal. Chocolate chip cookies don't lean on sugar; they don't depend on it for their very existence.

Other, more blatantly pandering foods rely on the cruder elements of the palate. They play, as it were, to the cheap seats in the theater, satisfying only basic, coarse needs. As in, "My sweet tooth is cloyed only by ingesting a dozen Three Musketeers bars in a half-hour," or "My idea of Nirvana is sole possession of a two-pound lollipop." For those among us who so love sugar, the chocolate chip cookie must prove a disappointment. Put differently, the sweetness of a chocolate chip cookie is a relative sensation. A matter of subjective appreciation. It is a mixed delight. A matter of degree. Part, but only part, of the whole.

Which is why sugar is so important in a cookie. It can overstate itself, take control and run riot, thereby messing up everything.

So, chocolate chip cookies should be made with carefully measured amounts of sugars. Almost all recipes call for some amount of white, granulated sugar. This is the normal, gritty sugar you put in coffee or tea. It's just sugar. Everybody's sugar. Bleached, pure white and sweet. In executing a recipe add neither more nor less than requested unless you are involved in an experimental batch.

Brown sugar, on the other hand, is entirely different. In rare instances it is the sugar from cane or beets that hasn't been processed into a profound state of colorlessness. In the unlikely event you can find really "pure" brown sugar, you'll be delighted to discover the richness of its taste. And its flavor is decidedly semi-sweet. Most of us, however, will buy brown sugar that is really extra-coarse, white, granulated sugar with added molasses. Dark brown sugar has a mild molasses added, endowing the sugar with a relatively strong flavor that mitigates, slightly, the sugar. Light brown sugar includes an even milder molasses, this lighter syrup having a less pronounced influence on the sweetness of the basic sugar involved.

Sugar, in all its disguises, is important to cookies beyond the sweetness it adds to them. It also increases the tenderness, the fragility of taste in a cookie. It makes them somewhat gentler.

Honey, on the other hand, makes cookies wet. If you are interested in honey, or feel compelled to experiment with it, be sure to substitute about three-quarters the amount of sugar called for when using honey. If there's any liquid required, such as milk, reduce it slightly as well.

Butter.

Very few people who bother to think about it feel indifferent about butter. One is either bonkers over the stuff or, it seems, feels negative toward it. Some, this writer included, feel that rolls, corn on the cob, toast and potatoes are excellent foods to eat with butter. Which is to say, these foods are appreciated primarily because they justify the consumption of terrific quantities of churned dairy fats. Emotional imbalances of this kind almost never can be corrected and so, why bother trying?

Butter is made by churning, or agitating, cream until the oils in it have formed separate globs. The resulting semi-solid stuff is 80% fat and 20% water and milk solids. It's very creamy colored, not nearly as yellow as the butter sold in stores, and has a mild, delicate flavor. The butter you buy also contains a

Butter lover.

certain amount of coloring and may or may not have salt added to it for flavor and as a preservative. Generally speaking, true butter lovers prefer unsalted butter.

But many cookie lovers consider the taste that butter lends to a chocolate chip cookie less important than the texture it supplies. And there is a sizable minority that strongly prefers the texture of a cookie made with margarine instead of butter. The difference, of course, comes from the different fats in the two foods. Margarine is made from vegetable oils with a dash of dairy and/or animal fats sometimes added. Margarine is better for you than butter and gives cookies a texture that can be described (depending on your perspective) as either bland or tender.

Vegetable shortening is basically vegetable oils that are whipped up to introduce air into them. The white, frothy stuff is then deodorized, colored and loaded into tins. Vegetable shortening is added to batter by those who prefer very light cookies. It normally replaces only a portion of the butter or margarine otherwise included.

Chocolate.
The human mind has struggled for centuries with a few seemingly simple issues. Questions of war and peace, the true distinction between good and evil, the nature and existence of a deity and the blending of the ideal chocolate have proven eternally compelling challenges. Despite the enormity and apparent futility of resolving such imponderables, we keep trying, driven by the overwhelming significance of the matters at hand.

And, indeed, chocolate ultimately may prove to be the most difficult of all possible issues. After all, chocolate is the Big Magoo. It is The Ingredient. It is the Fred Astaire of the cookie world. The Eiffel Tower of baking. The Cole Porter of oven harmonies. Chocolate delights the palate, stirs the emotions and separates the truly sophisticated gourmet from those who eat to live. But most important, chocolate is the magic that distinguishes chocolate chip cookies from all other edibles. Thus, a full understanding of it is essential to mastering the baking of our treat.

The cocoa tree grows only in tropical climates. Its fruit, strange-looking green and maroon things about the size and shape of summer squash, contain about 35 seeds each. These beans, creamy lavender and about one inch long, are the raw material from which chocolate is made. The entire process is long and complicated but can be summed up.

The beans are air-dried, causing them to ferment slightly and turn a dark brown. Then different beans are blended, fumigated, sieved, cleaned, weighed, roasted, cooled, shelled and crushed. This mashing liquefies the fats, or butter, in the cocoa and most of it is removed. What's left is a thick, dark paste known as chocolate liquor.

This liquor is what most of us know as baking chocolate. If it is mixed with a little cocoa butter, sugar and vanilla and then churned to blend these ingredients, emulsify the liquids and break up the sugar crystals, semi-sweet chocolate is produced. Now, there is an almost infinite variety of ways to proportion and mix liquor, cocoa butter and sugar. And so there are many different kinds of "semi-sweet" chocolate. Some of them are quite bitter since they contain relatively little sugar, while others are very sweet indeed. All that you know for sure when you buy

Chocolate chip cookies are the Fred Astaires of the cookie world.

semi-sweet chocolate is that it contains between 15% and 35% pure chocolate liquor.

Bittersweet chocolate, on the other hand, contains as much as 50% liquor and very little sugar. It is a heady, intense kind of chocolate appreciated by real aficionados.

Some chocolates are "Dutch processed." This means that a minuscule amount of alkali is added to the chocolate to neutralize some of the acids in the liquor, making the chocolate less bitter. The process also tends to darken the chocolate.

Milk chocolate contains about 10% liquor, cocoa butter, sugar and vanilla, but also has milk solids in it. Milk chocolate is a candy, or more properly a *food*, not an ingredient. It has absolutely no business whatsoever getting anywhere near a chocolate chip cookie.

A strange material known as "white" chocolate is made from cocoa butter, sugar, milk and flavoring. Note that the essence of chocolate, the liquor, is omitted entirely. What's more, the flavoring in white chocolate includes things like lecithin, vanillin and whey powder. It is impossible to imagine the demented soul who would willfully add anything called lecithin to a homemade chocolate chip cookie.

Along these same lines, you may at one time or another stumble upon something called carob. This impostor is the powdered fruit of a Mediterranean tree. It happens to be brown. When mixed with vegetable fats and sugar it has the same general texture as chocolate. It even cooks the same way. So what.

Chocolate should be stored in a cool, dry place at about 65°F. It can be kept in the refrigerator, providing you seal it in an airtight container to keep other flavors from insinuating themselves into the chocolate. And remember to leave the chocolate sealed until it has reached room temperature again or it will "sweat." That is, moisture will condense on it. At temperatures over 85°F, chocolate "blooms." This means that some of the cocoa butter it contains separates from the sugar and liquor, and rises to the surface of the chocolate to form a thin, grey coating. This pale covering is perfectly harmless and will disappear as soon as your chocolate is cooked.

The chocolate world is made up of a great number of

different chocolates. Some have the quality and pizzazz of a Ferrari, while others are as pedestrian as a sleepy paperboy. And judging chocolates is like picking a spouse: it's a highly subjective process. But there are some things you should look for when you select a chocolate for your cookies. Be sure the stuff smells very chocolatey. This is an important element in making your kitchen an unspeakably beautiful place to be in while your cookies are cooling. Also, chocolate shouldn't be too sweet. Rather, it should contrast slightly with the sugar in your cookies. And finally, it shouldn't be too brittle. When your cookies cool to room temperature, a brittle, splintery chocolate won't lend them the touch of softness they need.

Baking Soda and Powders. Baking powder is like artificial yeast. It's amazing and a little goes a long way. Basically, baking powder works by combining an acid and an alkali in the presence of moisture. When this happens carbon dioxide gas is produced. And it's this gas, being manufactured inside your cookies, that bubbles through the batter. Of course, when the cookie is cooked the bubbles are trapped, creating the crumbliness so necessary to any baked goods.

The differences between baking powders lie in how fast they work. Tartrate baking powder and phosphate baking powder are both relatively quick-acting. As soon as they come in contact with the moisture in your batter, they begin giving off gases. Thus, you have to mix them into the batter and cook immediately thereafter. S.A.S. baking powders, known as "double-acting," work very little in cold batter. They are essentially activated by the heat of cooking. Thus, the work they do for your cookies isn't lost if you proceed slowly.

Baking soda operates under the same principle as powder, the combining of an acid and an alkali. But soda is used when there is an acid already present in a recipe, such as with chocolate chip cookies. Baking soda produces very tender, small crumbs and also tends to neutralize some of the bitterness in any cookie.

Vanilla.

The real cost of the small amount of vanilla in a batch of chocolate chip cookies is very slight. Therefore, it seems to me a bit odd that anyone would use "imitation" vanilla rather than "pure extract." That's all I have to say on the matter.

Other Ingredients.

As has been mentioned, the chocolate chip cookie is a sturdy creation. It has gumption, integrity, the right stuff. And for just this reason it can be very successfully tampered with in a wide variety of ways. Substitutions and additions of all kinds are possible. In fact, their number is probably only limited by your imagination and your ability to eat your failures.

What follows is a simple listing of the most popular additives that can be mixed into chocolate chip cookie batter. Please note that this is not a grouping of suggested alternatives to the classic cookie. You have here nothing more nor less than a report on a variety of materials that are known to have been added to a chocolate chip cookie without apparent harm to those who then ate them. From there, you're on your own.

Chocolate chip cookies sometimes contain one or more of the following: raisins, chopped dates, shredded coconut, coconut extract, crushed Wheaties, Rice Crispies, crumbled graham crackers, mashed potato chips, maraschino cherries, mashed banana, allspice, cream cheese, sour cream, crushed peppermint sticks, molasses, granola, coffee, chopped prunes, every edible nut, grated orange rind, chopped candied orange peel, candied ginger, pumpkin seeds, wheat germ, cinnamon, honey, nutmeg, lemon rind, lemon juice, orange juice, oatmeal, peanut butter, sunflower seeds and almond extract.

An Everyday How-To

MIXING AND BAKING chocolate chip cookies is a straightforward affair, completely bereft of complexity and lacking almost all forms of subtlety. Anyone, absolutely anyone, who can read can bake terrific chocolate chip cookies.

However, the very first time you make them, you are likely to stumble over a few technical details in the process. You'll probably take too long to do something. You'll forget a step or omit an ingredient. One way or another, most people foul up their first batch of cookies. An experience of this sort is akin to swallowing salt water the first time you try to swim. It's a little like bungling your first kiss. There's nothing wrong with you and there's nothing wrong with the cookies. All you need is a little practice.

It's important to note that there are no secrets in the cookie business. No arcane skills are required. Rather, the problem is a matter of developing a certain ease, a kind of facility with the whole endeavor. Doing so requires a decent amount of patience and a few hints. Patience, I'm sorry to say, doesn't come in book form. But hints do. So, what follows is a more or less chronological litany of considerations, tips and half-useful clues to baking the perfect chocolate chip cookie. Think of it as a check list that you ought to read shortly before your first batch of cookies and immediately after your third batch.

REGARDLESS of the essential reasonableness of recipe writers, people insist on altering perfectly good instructions. Among the most likely forms of tampering is the division or multiplication of a recipe to yield more or fewer cookies. As you know, many, many recipes for foods other than chocolate chip cookies don't take kindly to this sort of abuse. And they rebel in a tried-and-true fashion: the recipes won't work. But cookies don't seem to be so hypersensitive. Generally, you can cut everything in half and get perfectly good cookies just the same. And doubling a recipe is not only a good idea, it works even better.

But, if you're going to play games with a recipe in this book, do so well in advance. That is, sit down with a pencil and paper and make your reduction or multiplication. Create a brand-new recipe, written down. Trying to do long division in your head, from memory while a beater is turning, will never work.

ASSEMBLE all your ingredients before

you begin. Which is to say, be sure you have them handy. Put each and every one on the counter top right before your very eyes.

Doing so accomplishes three things: first, you know in advance that you have what you need. Second, it puts all the ingredients within arm's reach so that you don't have to scurry about searching for something. And third, if all your basic materials are to your right before you add them to your batter and you put them to your left when you have done so, there will never be any question in your mind what has been loaded into the mix and what has not.

IF YOU HAVE refrigerated your chocolate bars or chips, remove them from their chilly confines at least a half-hour before you want to begin mixing batter. And then leave them in their sealed, airtight plastic bag or box until they have reached room temperature. Cold chocolate gathers moisture, in the form of condensed droplets, if it is allowed to warm in the open air.

WITH APLOMB, unroll, tear off and position two piles of wax paper squares. Each sheet should measure approximately 18 inches on a side and each pile should have two sheets in it. This slippery paper will be used to hold sifted flour, will gather ingredients to be added to your batter and will protect your counter top. You don't really need four sheets, but having the wax paper available will make you feel self-confident.

AS EVERYONE KNOWS, there are several manufacturers of chocolate chips, morsels, bits, what-have-you. These are wonderful things, even cute. Great for sneaking a nibble and convenient when making cookies. But sooner or later you're probably going to want to experiment with chopping up your own chocolate bar. This may occur because you think that irregularly shaped chips might be fun. Or, you may develop a real taste for some particularly exotic chocolate. Irrespective of your motivation, be sure to chop your chocolate in advance. Make sure it's cool, not cold, when you begin. Then, using a sharp knife with a curved blade, rock the knife back and forth over the bar, cutting it up. Don't mince the chocolate. And don't carve it into simple, huge hunks. Chop it up so that each piece is about a quarter of an inch square. Then put the chunks in a small glass dish, out of the sun, off to the side.

NOT ALL chocolate chip cookies contain nuts. But most of them do. And so you should break up or chop up your selected nuts in advance. People have been known to use knives, their fingers and even rolling pins to make large nuts smaller.

DEPENDING on how quick you are with the basic ingredients of a cookie and how adept with a mixer, this is probably the point at which you should preheat your oven. First, divide your oven into thirds by positioning two racks in it. (Note that purists cook cookies using only one cookie sheet, while the rest of us can't stand waiting so long.) Then put your oven thermometer in the center of the lower rack and close the oven door.

After about ten minutes check the thermometer. It will, guaranteed, read some temperature other than that which you have set. Adjust your oven accordingly, disregarding the temperature you seem to be requesting, until you actually get the oven to the heated level you require.

AT THIS POINT you must perform the single most difficult act of a chocolate chip cookie baker's career. You must pause. Stop. Avoid hurrying by momentarily doing nothing at all.

This bit of advice may seem gratuitous to you. But there is nothing on earth that chocolate chip cookie batter abhors more than haste. Somehow it can sense impatience. To an alarming extent it absorbs disquietude. Assimilates worry. Adopts the spirit of the frenetic and rebels as a result. So go slowly. Your cookies will repay the extra time you've invested with ample dividends. Next, cut several sheets of aluminum foil to fit your cookie sheets. This tip, obviously, is optional. Lots of people use butter or bee's wax or flour or very finely crushed bread crumbs to keep their cookies from sticking to cookie sheets. However, cookies with lots of butter in them, such as chocolate chip cookies, tend to spread out on a buttered cookie sheet. If you like large, thin cookies, this result is just fine. But most folks prefer slightly stouter cookies and aluminum foil helps achieve this.

Aluminum foil is also useful because you don't have to cool your cookie sheets between bakings. Instead, while one batch of cookies is baking, you can put dollops of batter on a sheet of aluminum foil, in preparation. When batch number one has baked, simply slip the aluminum foil off the sheets and slide on the new foil, containing batch number two. After removing the cookies from the aluminum foil and putting them on a rack, wipe the used foil dry with a paper towel. It will cool quickly and will be ready for a new batch in a few minutes.

AT THIS POINT, strain your brown sugar. That is, using a strainer and your fingertips, force an ample supply of sugar through the mesh. This breaks up any clumps that may have formed. It doesn't, however, change the volume of the sugar when you measure it. Unlike flour, sugar should be pressed firmly into its measuring cup when you mete it out.

NOW, SIFT a healthy amount (meaning more than enough) of flour onto a sheet of wax paper. If you have a sifter with three screens, one sifting is enough. Otherwise, sift it twice. Then, gently measure the amount of flour called for and put it in the sifter. If you intend to sift baking soda and/or powder into the flour, as opposed to adding it mixed with water, add it to the flour now. Finally, sift these two together onto a clean piece of wax paper and put it all aside.

Flour is very heavy when compacted in a paper bag.

Note that you don't have to wash the sifter when you're done. Just shake loose flour off and put it away.

YOU'VE NOW COME to the magic moment when you actually get to start performing useful functions. Put differently, you get to do some stirring.

Regardless of whether you are using an electric mixer or creaming your butter by hand, it's easier if the butter is at room temperature. If not, the process will take a little longer. However, be sure you go slowly, using the slowest speed on any mixer. The point here is to stir the butter until it is thick and viscous, a kind of almost-liquid-but-not-quite.

GENERALLY speaking, the first thing added to creamed butter is sugar. As has been mentioned, use metal measuring cups for all the dry ingredients you use. But, when measuring sugar you should press the stuff firmly into the cup before leveling the top. Sugar isn't measured light and fluffy like flour.

IF YOU ARE substituting honey for any of the sugar called for, use about ¾ as much honey, by volume, as the sugar you omit.

Substitute odd sorts of eggs for hens' eggs with some care.

IN ALMOST ALL recipes the next thing added to the developing batter is eggs. Use large or extra-large eggs. Break them into a small glass bowl, not into your mixing bowl. Plopping them first into a container of their own will make it easier for you to check whether bits of eggshell have fallen in as well. After you've inspected and cleared any shell chips from the eggs, pour the eggs into the mixing bowl.

SOME FOLKS like rich cookies, others prefer them light and airy. If you enjoy chocolate chip cookies when they resemble cake more than pastry, you might try adding an extra egg yolk to your batter. If the recipe calls for two large eggs, add the yolk of one medium-sized egg.

To do this, of course, you have to separate the yolk from the white of the egg. This is an eternally interesting process. First, you need two bowls. Then holding the egg in one hand, rap it firmly against the rim of one of the bowls so that it cracks about halfway through at the midline of the egg. Next, with this crack facing up and with one end of the egg in your left hand and one end in your right hand, hold the thing over one of the bowls. Then pry the shell apart with your thumbs, lowering the larger half of the shell as you do so to form a kind of bowl that will hold the yolk.

This will cause egg white to ooze out of the shell, falling, hopefully, into the bowl below. It will, of course, glop up your fingers along the way. Having become reasonably gooey, the rest is easy. You simply pour the egg yolk back and forth between the two half eggshells, letting egg white drip into the bowl as you do so. Eventually, all the white will separate from the yolk. Then drop the yolk into your second bowl, inspect it for shell bits and, finally, add it to your other eggs.

NEXT, add vanilla. After you've done so, be sure to seal the bottle tightly as the alcohol and water in vanilla extract evaporates quickly, stealing some of the taste in the process.

MIX ALL of this together using the slowest speed on your mixer. Be thorough, making sure that everything is evenly distributed throughout the batter. But don't overwork the mixture. It will make your cookies tough.

AT THIS POINT the flour is called for. With your mixer at low speed you should add the flour gradually to your batter. Use a spatula to scrape the unmixed flour from the side of your mixing bowl and work it into the beaters. But don't mix this nearly complete batter any longer than you have to in order to blend the flour with the other ingredients.

AS HAS BEEN mentioned elsewhere in this book, there are a couple of ways of adding baking soda to chocolate chip cookie mix. The vast majority of cooks sift it into their flour and so it is added to the batter along with the flour. But there are others who seem to feel that the stuff should be thoroughly moistened before going into the batter. (Note that this is the case only with soda, not baking

Measure baking soda carefully.

powder. The powder will begin working, to some extent at least, as soon as it comes in contact with water. Baking soda requires heat in order to work and so can be moistened in advance.) People who like to wet their baking soda do so by dissolving it in about a teaspoon of hot (not boiling) water. This soup is then added to the batter when about half the flour has been mixed in.

Among the jillions of variables that exist within the simple procedures for making chocolate chip cookies, this detail seems to be the most baffling. On the one hand, it makes perfect sense to water down your baking soda to be sure all of it will activate. But, on the other hand, I've never been able to perceive any difference in the cookies made using either method.

MIXING chocolate morsels, nuts, raisins and any other tidbits that you plan to throw into your batter should be done by hand. That is, don't use the electric mixer. And stir all this in gently, churning away only until your batter is mixed.

AT THIS POINT your batter is made. However, contrary to what you may expect, there are three things that you can do with it now. The first and most popular avenue is to sample it raw. Please note that the verb "to sample" is defined as taking a *small* segment that is judged as representative of the whole. You don't *have* to eat a third of a pound of raw batter in order to be certain it is worthy of your oven.

Of course, the second thing that can be done with raw batter is bake it into cookies.

But there is a third option, one that is extremely difficult to manage, requiring the self-discipline of a yogi, the iron will of a Titan. It involves covering your mixing bowl with plastic wrap and refrigerating the batter for twelve hours or so. This painful step in the cookie-making process was originated by Ruth Wakefield, the inventor of the chocolate chip cookie. Her theory was that the batter should sit a while so that the several tastes of the various ingredients could insinuate themselves into each other, blending into a subtle symphony. And, should you ever manage the feat of trying her technique, you probably will be surprised to discover that it works.

Beware, however, the inevitable attrition that unguarded chocolate chip cookie batter suffers when left to its own defenses in a refrigerator.

ASSUMING that your cookie sheets are either lightly greased with unsalted butter or have a sheet of aluminum foil over them, it is time to turn batter into cookies. It should be noted at this juncture that chocolate chip cookies are one of a large number of cookies generally referred to as "drop" cookies. They have been so named because one is supposed to spoon a blob of batter from the mixing bowl and then drop it onto a cookie sheet. Now, anyone who has ever made chocolate chip cookies knows that the batter won't ever drop off the spoon. It has to be coerced, even pried off. So if you ever read about or hear someone mention "dropping" cookies, offer up a hearty but good-natured chuckle of ridicule. Cookies don't drop.

ABSOLUTE FACT: the bigger the mound of batter on the cookie sheet, the bigger the cookie it will produce.

THERE ARE TWO ways to get batter from a bowl onto a cookie sheet. The first is to spoon it on, usually employing two teaspoons, one to lift the batter and the other to scrape it off the first spoon.

An easier way, in my opinion, is to roll batter into balls with the palms of your hands. This isn't difficult to do as long as you keep your hands either wet or lightly coated with powdered sugar. After you've positioned the balls on the cookie sheet, press them a bit with the bottom of a spoon so they flatten out a little.

POSITION YOUR cookies far enough apart on the sheet so that they don't run together. Since different recipes "spread" differently and since no two people put exactly the same amount of batter into a cookie, you'll have to experiment in order to be sure you won't get Siamese cookies. That is, cookies that are all stuck together. But start placing your blobs about two inches apart.

IF IN YOUR last batch of cookies you don't have enough batter to fill a cookie sheet using your normal spacing, increase the spacing. That is, fill the sheet completely even if you have to put the cookies four or five inches apart. Totally covering the sheet insures that all the cookies will bake evenly.

AS HAS BEEN discussed elsewhere, there are several different types of "basic" cookie batter. These, based on different proportions of ingredients, produce different kinds of cookies. But the mix of ingredients in your cookies isn't the only operating factor determining the product of your labors. The baking makes a difference, too.

Lower heat levels, such as 300-325°F, applied for a relatively longer period of time, produce what can only be described as hard cookies. In fact, to most tastes this can only be considered a charitable description. Actually, the things are white, chalky little pellets that aren't worth eating.

Higher oven temperature levels, between 350-375°F, and somewhat shorter cooking times, tend to produce crispy, golden cookies. Straight from the oven they're still moist and flexible but hold their shape very well.

Very high heat levels, around 400°F, applied for short periods, result in cookies that are variously described as soft and chewy or underbaked, limp and soggy.

Store cookies in a cool, dry place.

ALL CHOCOLATE chip cookies taste best when they are fresh from the oven. However, they store reasonably well when frozen in an airtight container such as a plastic freezer box. While it's almost impossible to imagine anyone managing to avoid homemade cookies for two weeks when they beckon within arm's reach, don't leave them frozen much longer even if you can. And when it comes time to thaw the cookies, do so by leaving them in their sealed containers. Cold cookies condense moisture on their surfaces if thawed in the open air and this water can make them soggy.

ON THE OTHER HAND, if your cookies dry out in a cookie jar somewhere, dampen a paper towel and drop it in the jar. In a couple of hours your cookies will be remoisturized.

ONE FINAL NOTE about cooking cookies. It is entirely possible to bake chocolate chip cookies in the same way many of us fry bacon on Sunday mornings. That is, you can do so slowly, in small batches, allowing plenty of time for the sole cookie sheet you're using to cool between bakings. This method is a wonderfully relaxing form of recreation. However, it is often a process similar to filling a very large, very powerful automobile with gasoline while leaving the engine running. You may, in the end, have absolutely nothing to show for your efforts.

An Introduction to the Recipes

IT HAS BEEN estimated that enough trees to forest Saudi Arabia have sacrificed their lives so that cookbooks might be published. Which is to say that you are now holding in your hands but one small effort in a long and noble tradition. And, since this is the introduction to the recipe section of a cookbook, there is a definite and well-established form to be followed here. Certain observations concerning the food in question ought to be made. Much good-humored encouragement should be offered. A few myths must be debunked. And finally you are to be cautioned never, ever to break the rules by failing to follow a recipe *exactly*.

This last bit of advice, however, seems to me to be pompously self-righteous. I'm sympathetic to those chefs and writers who cannot resist telling readers that their recipes are perfect. After all, we who write this sort of information test and retest everything until we never want to see the food again. We overresearch our efforts and tinker with our suggested recipes until the cows come home. And all this goes on until pure pride sends a shudder down the spine of anyone who hears that a dash of pepper has been added to his favorite soup concoction.

But a proper introduction to the chocolate chip cookie really shouldn't alarm the public concerning the precision with which it must be baked. A true paean to America's favorite snack, an accurate and honest ode to those chewy disks we all know and love, ought to let you know that a chocolate chip cookie is spectacularly easy to make. A cinch. No problem.

In order to prove this obvious contention, the authors employed the calculating capacity of a sizable computer to analyze the contents of a whole bunch of different chocolate chip cookie recipes. And, having tabulated the results, we can now report that no two of them are exactly the same but that they're all more or less alike.

Chocolate chip cookies are made using flour, butter and sugar as a basic batter. To this one adds eggs, vanilla, salt, baking soda and chocolate bits of some kind. Voilà, the chocolate chip cookie. Naturally, people put other things in their batter. Lots of other things. And this sort of tampering makes their cookies interesting. It even makes them better, sometimes. But the basic cookie remains, supporting and sustaining all the additives that the fertile imaginations of people who cook can think up.

This observation, that the basic chocolate chip cookie is a reliable creation, is very comforting. Once you've settled on a recipe for cookies that not only works but renders you results you genuinely like eating, you can feel free to experiment. There are very few things that can be added to chocolate chip cookies that actually will make them inedible. So, even if you aren't thrilled with some experimental flights of fancy, you still probably won't mind eating what you've made. Very few concoctions that come out of a kitchen can make such a claim.

There is, however, one crucial area of consideration that you should know about. It is the question of proportion among the ingredients flour, butter and sugar. These three elements of a cookie determine much of its basic character. So it is mightily important that you decide what sort of cookies you like and what relative proportions of these three will create it for you.

But offering you some tips about the three architecturally critical parts of a cookie's framework isn't easy. The area is fraught with bias and interpretation. For everyone likes their chocolate chip cookies just so. Just the way they remember them. Still, in order to re-create whatever ideal cookie floats in your memory, you should know a few simple, highly subjective facts. First, the more butter (or margarine or shortening) you put in a cookie, the chewier, gooier, moister and more bendable it will be. It also will flatten out when cooked, making it thinner. The more flour you add, the more cakey, crispy, light and thick it will be. And sugar, of course, makes things sweeter.

Having fulfilled my responsibility concerning all the important cautionary notes that should preface a series of recipes, I now ask that you try the recipes here as they are presented at least once. Thereafter, feel free to tamper with them to your heart's content. And, should you find that you've come up with something really terrific, please send it to us. Since the authors fervently hope that this book will be so popular that a revised and expanded second edition will be demanded by our impatient fans, we'd like to invite you to send us your cookie recipes. No prizes, awards, benefits, royalties or fame are offered in return. We'll just credit you in very small type if your recipe is published.

Send your recipe to:

Bob & Suzanne Stat
Banbury Books
37 West Avenue
Wayne, Pennsylvania 19087

Blonde Brownies

2 cups unsifted all-purpose flour
1 teaspoon double-acting baking powder
1 teaspoon salt
¼ teaspoon baking soda
⅔ cup butter or margarine
2 cups brown sugar, firmly packed
2 eggs, lightly beaten
2 teaspoons vanilla extract
1 cup semi-sweet chocolate chips
⅓ cup chopped walnuts

Oven temperature: 350°F

Mix flour with baking powder, salt and soda. Melt butter in a saucepan and add sugar. Blend in eggs and vanilla. Add flour mixture, a small amount at a time, mixing well after each addition. Spread in an ungreased 13" x 9" pan. Sprinkle with chocolate chips and nuts. Bake 30 minutes. Cool in pan, then cut into bars. Makes 48 bars.

Thanks to General Foods

Original Toll House® Cookies

2¼ cups unsifted flour
1 measuring teaspoon baking soda
1 measuring teaspoon salt
1 cup butter, softened
¾ cup granulated sugar
¾ cup brown sugar, firmly packed
1 measuring teaspoon vanilla extract
2 eggs
1 12-ounce package Nestlé's Semi-Sweet Real Chocolate Morsels
1 cup chopped nuts

Oven temperature: 375°F

In a small bowl, combine flour, baking soda and salt; set aside. In a large bowl, combine butter, sugar, brown sugar and vanilla extract; beat until creamy. Beat in eggs. Gradually add flour mixture; mix well. Stir in Nestlé's Semi-Sweet Real Chocolate Morsels and nuts. Drop by rounded measuring teaspoonful onto ungreased cookie sheets. Bake at 375°F for 8-10 minutes. Makes 100 2-inch cookies.

Toll House® Pan Cookie: To make the quick Toll House® Pan Cookie, spread the original Toll House® Cookie dough into a greased 15" x 10" x 1" baking pan. Bake at 375°F for 20 minutes. Cool; cut into 35 2-inch squares.

© The Nestlé Company

Chocolate Chip Cheesecake

For the crust, combine:
 1 cup flour
 3 tablespoons granulated sugar
 ¼ teaspoon salt
 ¼ cup unsweetened cocoa

Cut in:
 ½ cup cold unsalted butter

Press crust mixture into the bottom of a 9" x 3" cheesecake or springform pan that has been greased and floured. Bake at 350°F for 25 minutes. Cool.

For the filling, cream:
 1½ pounds softened cream cheese
 1¼ cups sugar

Beat together and add:
 1½ cups sour cream
 3 eggs
 1 teaspoon vanilla
 ½ teaspoon salt

Fold in:
 6 ounces miniature chocolate chips

Pour into the crust and bake at 325°F for 1 hour. Cool.

For the topping, combine:
 1½ cups sour cream
 1 teaspoon vanilla extract
 2 tablespoons sugar

Spread over the cooled cheesecake and bake for 5-7 minutes at 425°F. Cool and then chill overnight before removing from the pan.

Thanks to The Commissary, Philadelphia, Pa.

Suzanne's Favorite Cookies

2¼ cups unsifted flour
1 teaspoon baking soda
½ teaspoon salt
1 cup butter
¾ cup granulated sugar
¾ cup brown sugar, firmly packed
1 teaspoon vanilla extract
2 eggs, lightly beaten
12 ounces semi-sweet chocolate chips
2 tablespoons Grand Marnier
1 tablespoon grated orange rind

Oven temperature: 375°F

Sift flour, baking soda and salt. In a separate bowl, cream butter and sugars. Add vanilla, eggs, Grand Marnier and orange rind; beat well. Combine flour mixture with liquid mixture and blend all ingredients. Fold in chocolate chips. Drop by tablespoon onto greased or foil-covered cookie sheets. Bake 10-12 minutes or until golden. Makes 4½ dozen large cookies.

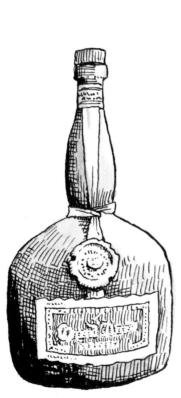

Brownies

4 *squares unsweetened chocolate*
1 *cup butter*
2 *cups granulated sugar*
4 *large eggs*
1 *cup flour*
2 *cups miniature marshmallows*
6 *ounces semi-sweet chocolate chips*
1 *cup chopped walnuts*
1 *tablespoon rum*
Dash salt

Oven temperature: 350°F (325°F if using a glass pan)

In a large bowl, melt chocolate squares and butter. Add sugar. Beat in eggs, one at a time. Stir in flour. Add remaining ingredients and stir. Pour into a 9" x 11" pan. Bake 35-45 minutes or until barely done and still moist inside. Allow to sit overnight covered or refrigerate. Serve at room temperature.

Calendar Cookies

½ cup butter or margarine
½ cup granulated sugar
½ cup brown sugar, firmly packed
1 egg
1 teaspoon vanilla extract
1¼ cups flour
½ teaspoon baking soda
½ teaspoon baking powder
½ teaspoon salt
1¼ cups oats
1 cup chopped dates
12 ounces semi-sweet chocolate chips
¾ cup walnuts, chopped

Oven temperature: 375°F

Cream butter and sugars until light and fluffy. Beat in egg and vanilla. Sift together then combine flour, baking soda, baking powder and salt. Fold in oats, dates, chocolate chips and walnuts. Drop by teaspoon onto greased baking sheets. Bake 10-12 minutes. Makes 5 dozen cookies.

First, chop the dates . . .

Microwave Chocolate Cookies

6 *ounces semi-sweet chocolate chips*
½ *cup butter*
1½ *cups brown sugar*
4 *eggs*
2 *teaspoons vanilla*
3¾ *cups all-purpose flour*
1 *teaspoon cinnamon*
½ *teaspoon salt*
½ *cup chopped walnuts or shredded coconut*
Walnut halves

Microwave power level: High (100%)

Combine chocolate chips and butter in a large glass mixing bowl. Microwave on High (100%) for 1-1½ minutes or until melted. Stir halfway through cooking time. Add sugar, eggs and vanilla. Beat until well blended. Stir in dry ingredients until well blended. Chill dough for 2-3 hours. Shape into ¾" balls and roll in walnuts or coconut. Place desired amount of balls in a circle, 2" apart on waxed paper. Place a walnut half in the center of each and press down. Refrigerate leftover dough until ready to use. Microwave balls on High (100%) until set but still moist.

Amount	Time
1	45 seconds-1 minute
2	1-1¼ minutes
6	2-2¼ minutes

Allow cookies to stand for 3 minutes on a solid surface before removing from waxed paper. Makes 4-5 dozen cookies.

© The Tappan Company — 1979

David's Butterscotch Chocolate Chunk Cookies

1 cup *unsalted butter*
½ pound *brown sugar, firmly packed*
½ teaspoon *salt*
½ teaspoon *vanilla extract*
1 *large egg*
8 ounces *unbleached flour, by weight*
8 ounces *imported bittersweet chocolate, chopped roughly by hand*

Oven temperature: 400°F

Combine all ingredients except flour and chocolate in a mixer at medium speed, or beat together by hand in a bowl. Batter should be smooth and lump-free. Add flour and chocolate and mix until no traces of white flour can be seen in dough. Drop by heaping teaspoonful 2 inches apart on a cookie sheet that is either covered by nonstick silicone baking paper or is well buttered. Bake 6-8 minutes or until edges barely start to brown. Remove to wire rack to cool.

© David's Cookies

Chocolate Chip Sour Cream Cake

¼ pound butter
1 cup granulated sugar
2 eggs, beaten
2 cups flour
1 teaspoon baking soda
1 cup sour cream
2 tablespoons milk
1½ teaspoons vanilla extract
6 ounces semi-sweet chocolate chips
½ cup sugar
2 teaspoons cinnamon

Oven temperature: 375°F

Cream together butter and sugar. Beat in eggs until mixture is light and fluffy. Sift together flour and baking soda. Combine milk with sour cream. Into butter-sugar-egg mixture beat in part of the flour, then beat in some of the sour cream-milk mixture. Alternate until all are well combined. Add vanilla, then fold in chocolate chips. Pour half the batter into a greased and floured 10-inch tube pan. Mix sugar and cinnamon and sprinkle half the mixture onto the batter in the pan. Gently pour on remaining batter, then sprinkle remaining cinnamon and sugar. Bake 45 minutes. Allow to cool in the pan for about 2 hours before removing the cake.

Thanks to Lillian Sussman

German Chocolate Brownies

1 *package German chocolate cake mix*
⅓ *cup milk*
¼ *cup butter or margarine, softened*
1 *large egg*
6 *ounces semi-sweet chocolate chips*
6 *ounces chopped walnuts*

Oven temperature: 350°F

In a large mixing bowl, combine cake mix, milk, butter and egg. Fold in chocolate chips and nuts. Pour into greased and lightly floured 13″ x 19″ baking pan. Bake 20-30 minutes or until an inserted toothpick comes out clean. Cool, then cut into squares.

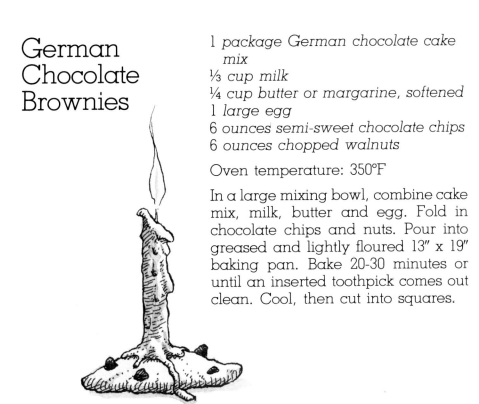

Crunchy Peanut Butter Balls

1 *cup creamy peanut butter*
⅔ *cup sweetened condensed milk*
1 *cup crunchy nutlike cereal nuggets*
¼ *cup semi-sweet chocolate chips*

Combine peanut butter, milk, ½ cup of cereal and chocolate chips in a bowl, mixing well. Chill 30 minutes, then roll into balls and roll balls in remaining cereal. Store in refrigerator. Makes 3½ dozen confections.

Thanks to General Foods

Breakfast Cookies

1 cup butter or margarine
1 cup granulated sugar
1 cup brown sugar, firmly packed
2 eggs
1 teaspoon vanilla extract
½ teaspoon salt
½ teaspoon baking soda
½ teaspoon baking powder
1 teaspoon cinnamon
1 cup oats
1 cup wheat flakes
2 cups sifted flour
12 ounces semi-sweet chocolate chips

Oven temperature: 350°F

Cream together butter and sugars. Add ingredients in order given; mix well. Drop by teaspoonful onto greased cookie sheets. Bake 10-12 minutes. Makes 3½ dozen cookies.

David's Lemon Chocolate Chunk Cookies

1 cup unsalted butter
½ cup granulated sugar
⅓ cup brown sugar, firmly packed
1 large egg
½ teaspoon pure vanilla extract
½ teaspoon salt
½ teaspoon baking soda
Grated rind of 2 lemons
Juice of 1 lemon (2 tablespoons)
7 ounces unbleached flour, by weight
8 ounces imported bittersweet
  chocolate, chopped roughly by
  hand

Oven temperature: 400°F

Combine all ingredients except flour and chocolate in a mixer at medium speed, or beat together by hand in a bowl. Batter should be smooth and lump-free. Add flour and chocolate and mix until no trace of white flour remains visible. Drop by heaping teaspoonful 2-3 inches apart onto a cookie sheet covered by nonstick baking paper. These cookies do not spread much. One heaping teaspoonful of dough will yield a cookie about two inches in diameter. For larger cookies, use rounded tablespoons of dough and space them 3 inches apart. Bake 7-8 minutes or until edges start to brown. Remove from pan while warm and let cool on wire rack.

© David's Cookies

Egad, Bogus Chip Cookies

1 cup sifted flour
½ teaspoon salt
½ teaspoon baking soda
½ cup butter or margarine, softened
½ cup granulated sugar
¼ cup dark brown sugar, firmly
  packed
1 egg, lightly beaten
1 teaspoon vanilla extract
½ cup semi-sweet chocolate chips
½ cup butterscotch chips
¾ cup chopped pecans

Oven temperature: 375°F

Sift flour, salt and baking soda; set aside. In a large mixing bowl, cream butter and sugars. Add egg and vanilla; blend well. Gradually add flour mixture, blending all ingredients. Fold in chocolate chips, butterscotch chips and pecans. Drop from a teaspoon onto greased cookie sheets. Bake 10-12 minutes or until lightly browned. Makes 3½ dozen cookies.

Mocha Peanut Clusters

1 *cup semi-sweet chocolate chips*
16 *large marshmallows, quartered*
⅓ *cup butter or margarine*
1 *tablespoon instant coffee*
2 *cups salted peanuts*

Combine chips, marshmallows and butter in the top of a double boiler. Cook over hot water, stirring occasionally until melted and smooth. Add instant coffee. Remove from heat and stir in peanuts. Drop from teaspoon onto waxed paper. Cool until firm. Makes 3 dozen clusters.

Santa Barbara Cookies

½ *cup sweet butter or margarine*
½ *cup granulated sugar*
⅓ *cup brown sugar*
1 *egg*
1 *teaspoon vanilla extract*
1 *cup sifted flour*
½ *teaspoon baking soda*
¼ *teaspoon salt*
6 *ounces semi-sweet chocolate chips*
⅓ *cup wheat germ, toasted or raw*
½ *cup chopped pecans*

Oven temperature: 375°F

Cream the butter with the sugars and blend well. Add egg (lightly beaten) and vanilla to mixture. Combine flour, baking soda and salt and mix until no trace of flour is visible. Fold in wheat germ, pecans and chocolate chips. Drop by teaspoon onto lightly buttered cookie sheets and bake 12 minutes. Makes 3½ dozen cookies.

Coffee Walnut Chocolate Chip Muffins

Cream together:
  ½ cup butter
  ½ cup brown sugar
  ½ cup granulated sugar
  3 tablespoons instant coffee
  2 teaspoons vanilla extract

In a separate bowl, beat together:
  2 eggs
  ⅔ cup milk

Combine:
  1¾ cups flour
  1 tablespoon baking powder
  ½ teaspoon salt

Alternately add the wet and dry ingredients to the butter mixture.

Stir in:
  ¾ cup semi-sweet chocolate chips
  1½ cups coarsely chopped walnuts

Grease and flour muffin tin. Pour in batter. Bake at 350°F for 20-25 minutes. Cool for 5 minutes before removing from tins. Makes 12 3-inch muffins.

Thanks to The Commissary, Philadelphia, Pa.

Sunshine Cookies

½ cup butter or margarine
⅓ cup granulated sugar
½ cup brown sugar, firmly packed
1 egg
1 teaspoon vanilla extract
1 tablespoon grated orange rind
1½ cups flour
½ teaspoon baking soda
½ teaspoon salt
1 cup oats
1 cup flaked coconut
12 ounces milk chocolate chips

Oven temperature: 375°F

Beat together butter and sugars until light and fluffy. Add egg, vanilla and orange rind and beat until well blended. Sift together flour, baking soda and salt and add to mixture, blending well. Fold in oats, coconut and chocolate chips. Drop by teaspoon onto greased cookie sheets and bake 10 minutes or until golden brown. Makes 3½ dozen cookies.

Killer Cake

This cake is best mixed by hand or mixed just to combine ingredients.

Melt over low heat, then cool to lukewarm:
> 6 ounces butter
> 6 ounces unsweetened chocolate

In a mixing bowl whisk together just to combine:
> 6 eggs
> 3 cups sugar
> ½ teaspoon salt (if using salted butter, decrease to ¼ teaspoon)
> 2 teaspoons vanilla extract

Stir in the butter and chocolate mix, then stir in:
> 1½ cups flour
> 1½ cups chocolate chips

Pour into two 9" x 1½" greased cake pans with removable bottoms, or line the bottom of the pans with waxed paper. Bake at 350°F for 30-40 minutes. You can tell when the cake is done by the puffiness on top with a few circular cracks. You can control the moistness of the cake by the amount of time it's baked. It will be more cakelike and less fudgy if baked for a longer period of time. Cool cake on racks and remove as soon as cooled. Wrap cake layers well if not frosted the same day.

Mocha Honey Frosting — Put in a mixing bowl and stir over low direct flame until chocolate is just melted:

  4 *ounces semi-sweet chocolate chips*
  ⅓ *cup honey*
  1 *tablespoon instant coffee*
  ¼ *cup water*

Remove from heat and cool to lukewarm, then whisk in:

  3 *egg yolks*

When combined add:

  3 *cups powdered sugar*

When smooth add:

  3 *ounces unsalted butter, room temperature*

To Assemble The Cake: Put one layer, bottom side up, on a cake plate. Spread it with ⅓ of the frosting. Top with the second layer of cake, bottom side up. Pour all but ½ cup or so of the frosting on top of the cake. Work the icing so that it overlaps the sides. Finish top, then finish sides. Use the ½ cup of reserved frosting to make 12 rosettes with pastry bag and open star tip over top of cake. Refrigerate if desired, but for best flavor and texture, serve at room temperature.

Thanks to The Commissary, Philadelphia, Pa.

Golden Gate Big Cookies

1 cup butter or margarine
1 cup granulated sugar
½ cup brown sugar, firmly packed
1 teaspoon vanilla extract
2 eggs
2½ cups flour
¾ teaspoon salt
½ teaspoon baking soda
12 ounces Guittard Milk Chocolate
    Chips

Oven temperature: 375°F

Cream together butter, sugars and vanilla. Add eggs and beat well. Sift together and add flour, salt and baking soda. Stir in Guittard Milk Chocolate Chips. Spread batter onto greased cookie sheet, making a round deposit four inches in diameter and ¼ inch or more thick. Use a knife or spoon. Form 2 batter deposits on a regular cookie sheet; this will allow cookies to spread to 6 inches during baking. Bake 12-15 minutes. Remove cookie sheet from oven and allow to cool one minute. Carefully remove Big Cookies from sheet using a large spatula. Makes 12 large cookies.

Thanks to Guittard Chocolate Company

Chocolate Bread

Combine 3 *packages active dry yeast* with ½ *cup warm water* (105°F) and 1 *teaspoon sugar.* Let proof.

Combine:
   12 *cups flour*
   1 *cup Dutch process cocoa*
   2 *tablespoons salt*
   14 *ounces small chocolate chips*
   ⅓ *cup sugar*

Add:
   Yeast mixture
   4 *cups warm water*
   1 *egg*
   1 *ounce shortening*

Mix and knead for 10 minutes, adding more flour or water if necessary. Put in greased bowl, cover with plastic wrap and let double in bulk. Punch down and divide into 3-4 pieces. Fold and shape into loaf pans or into round free-form loaves and place on a buttered baking sheet or let rise in a banneton and turn out on a buttered baking sheet. Cover and let rise until double. Bake in a 450°F oven for 15 minutes, reduce heat to 375°F and bake another 25 minutes until crusty and done.

© 1981, Williams-Sonoma

Almost Polyunsaturated Cookies

1 cup flour
½ teaspoon salt
½ teaspoon baking soda
½ cup butter
¼ cup granulated sugar
½ cup brown sugar, firmly packed
1 egg
1 teaspoon vanilla extract
6 ounces semi-sweet chocolate chips
½ cup raisins
½ cup toasted sunflower seeds

Oven temperature: 350°F

Sift together flour, salt and baking soda. In a separate bowl, cream together butter and sugars. Add egg and vanilla. Stir dry ingredients into mixture; blend well. Fold in chocolate chips, raisins and sunflower seeds. Drop by teaspoonful onto greased cookie sheets. Bake 10-12 minutes or until lightly browned. Makes 4 dozen cookies.

Famous Amos Raisin-Filled Chocolate Chip Cookies

1 cup margarine, softened
¾ cup firmly packed light brown sugar
¾ cup granulated sugar
1 teaspoon vanilla extract
1 teaspoon water
2 medium eggs
2½ cups sifted, all-purpose flour
1 teaspoon baking soda
½ teaspoon salt
2 cups raisins
1 12-ounce package semi-sweet chocolate pieces

Beat margarine, sugars, vanilla, water and eggs in a large bowl with electric mixer until creamy and thoroughly blended. With a spoon, stir in flour, baking soda and salt until well mixed. Stir in raisins and chocolate pieces. Spoon dough by teaspoonful onto cookie sheets. Allow 1 to 1½ inches between cookies for spreading. Bake at 375°F for 8 minutes, or until cookies are nicely browned, depending on how crisp or well done you like them. Makes about 6 dozen cookies.

©1975 TFACCCC

Toll House Chocolate Crunch Cookies

1 cup butter
¾ cup brown sugar
¾ cup white sugar
2 eggs, beaten
1 teaspoon vanilla extract
1 teaspoon baking soda
2¼ cups flour
1 teaspoon salt
1 cup chopped nuts
12 ounces semi-sweet chocolate
  morsels

Oven temperature: 375°F

Cream butter; add sugars, eggs and vanilla. Dissolve baking soda in one teaspoon hot water. Add alternately with flour to which salt has been added. Add nuts and chocolate morsels. Drop by half-teaspoonful onto greased cookie sheets. Bake 10-12 minutes. Makes 100 cookies.

NOTE: Along with this recipe, Mrs. Wakefield advises chilling the dough overnight, then rolling, by teaspoonful, into balls and placing two inches apart on greased baking sheets. Pressed lightly to form flat rounds, she notes, these cookies do not spread as much and keep a better shape.

From *Toll House Tried and True Recipes*, by Ruth Graves Wakefield, M. Barrows & Co., 1949

Granola Cookies

½ cup butter or margarine
⅓ cup granulated sugar
⅔ cup brown sugar, firmly packed
1 egg
1 teaspoon vanilla extract
1 cup flour
½ teaspoon salt
½ teaspoon baking soda
½ teaspoon baking powder
1 cup granola
1¼ cups mashed banana
6 ounces semi-sweet chocolate chips
½ cup chopped nuts

Oven temperature: 375°F

Beat butter with sugars until light and fluffy. Add egg and vanilla, beat well. Sift together and add flour, salt, baking soda, baking powder. Fold in granola, banana, chocolate chips and nuts. Drop by teaspoon onto greased cookie sheets. Bake 10-12 minutes or until lightly browned. Makes 4 dozen cookies.

Chocolate Chip Cream Cheese Dainties

½ cup butter
½ cup granulated sugar
3 ounces cream cheese
¼ teaspoon almond extract
1 cup sifted flour
½ teaspoon baking soda
½ teaspoon baking powder
¼ teaspoon salt
¾ cup chocolate chips
1 cup coarsely chopped crisp rice
  cereal

Oven temperature: 350°F

Cream together butter, cream cheese, sugar and almond extract. Stir in flour, baking soda, baking powder and salt. Add chocolate chips and mix lightly. Chill for 2-3 hours. Shape into small balls and roll in the cereal. Place on an ungreased cookie sheet. Top each cookie with a large chocolate chip or Wilbur bud. Bake 12-15 minutes. Makes 4 dozen cookies.

Thanks to The Wilbur Chocolate Company, Inc.

Bob's Weird But Lovable Cookies

1¼ cups unsifted flour
½ teaspoon baking soda
½ teaspoon salt
½ cup sweet butter
½ cup granulated sugar
¼ cup brown sugar, firmly packed
1 teaspoon vanilla extract
1 egg
¾ cup oats
½ cup semi-sweet chocolate chips
½ cup butterscotch chips
½ cup flaked coconut

Oven temperature: 375°F

Sift flour, salt and baking soda. In another bowl, cream together butter and sugars by hand or using an electric mixer. Beat in egg and vanilla. Combine flour mixture; blend well. Add by hand oats, chocolate chips, butterscotch chips and coconut. Drop by teaspoon onto greased cookie sheets. Bake 10-12 minutes. Makes 4 dozen cookies.

Doris Weatherminster's Favorites

1 cup flour
¼ teaspoon salt
¼ teaspoon baking soda
¼ teaspoon baking powder
½ cup butter or margarine, softened
1 cup brown sugar, firmly packed
1 tablespoon grated orange rind
1 carrot, grated
1½ teaspoons orange juice
1 egg
1 cup oats
¾ cup pecans, chopped
½ cup shredded coconut
6 ounces chocolate chips

Oven temperature: 350°F

In a large bowl, sift flour, salt, baking powder and soda. In a separate bowl, cream together butter and brown sugar. Beat in egg, orange rind and orange juice. Add flour mixture and carrot, oats, chocolate chips, pecans and coconut. Blend well. Drop by teaspoonful onto greased cookie sheets. Bake 12-15 minutes. Makes 3½ dozen cookies.

Sticks To The Roof Of Your Mouth Cookies

2¼ cups flour
1 teaspoon baking soda
½ teaspoon salt
1 teaspoon cinnamon
1 teaspoon nutmeg
1 cup butter or margarine
½ cup granulated sugar
¾ cup brown sugar, firmly packed
½ teaspoon vanilla extract
2 eggs
1 tablespoon orange juice
1 cup peanut butter
12 ounces milk chocolate chips
½ cup flaked coconut

Oven temperature: 375°F

Sift together flour, baking soda, salt, cinnamon and nutmeg; set aside. Cream butter with sugars, then add vanilla, eggs, orange juice and peanut butter. Beat until all ingredients are well blended. Add flour mixture and blend well. Fold in chocolate chips and coconut. Drop by teaspoon onto greased cookie sheets. Bake 10 minutes. Makes 4½ dozen cookies.

Chocolate Chip Squares

2 cups margarine, softened
1½ cups granulated sugar
1½ cups dark brown sugar, firmly
    packed
2 teaspoons vanilla extract
3 eggs
4½ cups unsifted flour
2 teaspoons baking soda
Dash salt
12 ounces chocolate chips

Oven temperature: 350°F

In a large bowl, blend the granulated sugar and margarine with a wooden spoon. Add the brown sugar and blend well. Beat in eggs by hand. Add baking soda and salt, then flour, and blend well. Fold in chocolate chips. Spread the mixture onto a lightly greased and floured 11" x 17" x 1" cookie sheet. Bake 30 minutes. Remove from oven and let cool for 10 minutes. Cut into 15 3½" x 3½" squares and let them cool on wire racks.

Thanks to Chowder House, Boothbay Harbor, Me.

Outrageously Hearty Cookies

1 cup whole wheat flour
½ teaspoon baking soda
½ teaspoon salt
¾ cup butter or margarine
1 cup brown sugar, firmly packed
½ cup granulated sugar
1 egg
1 tablespoon water
1 teaspoon vanilla extract
6 ounces semi-sweet chocolate chips
½ cup nuts, chopped
2½ cups oats
½ cup flaked coconut
2 tablespoons wheat germ

Oven temperature: 350°F

In a large bowl, mix whole wheat flour, baking soda and salt. Cream butter and sugars in a separate bowl. Add lightly beaten egg, water and vanilla. Stir flour mixture into liquid mixture. Gently fold in chocolate chips, nuts, oats, coconut and wheat germ. Drop by teaspoonful onto greased cookie sheets. Bake 12-15 minutes. Makes 4½ dozen cookies.

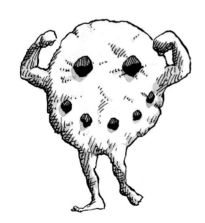

Chocolate Panettone

2 *packages active dry yeast*
⅓ *cup warm water (110°F)*
3 *cups flour*
¼ *cup sugar*
¼ *teaspoon salt*
3 *egg yolks*
2 *whole eggs*
1 *teaspoon vanilla extract*
2-3 *tablespoons rum*
Grated rind of 1 orange
4 *ounces unsalted butter, softened*
¼ *cup candied orange peel, finely chopped*
1 *cup small chocolate chips*

Oven temperature: 350°F

Dissolve yeast in the water, let foam, then mix with ½ cup of the flour. Form into a ball, put in a bowl, cover and set in a warm place for 30 minutes. Put rest of the flour in a large bowl; add sugar, salt, egg yolks, whole eggs, vanilla, rum, grated orange rind and mix all together; then add previously made ball of dough and knead. Add the softened butter and continue to knead until it is a smooth, soft and silky dough. (If sticky, add a little flour.) Now knead in candied orange peel and chocolate chips. Cover and let rise until double (about 1 hour). Punch down and put into well-buttered mold. Let rise until double (about 1 hour) and bake 30-35 minutes. Remove from oven, turn out on a baking sheet and glaze with a mixture of 1 egg beaten with ¼ cup sugar and ½ cup ground almonds. Dust with powdered sugar and sprinkle with slivered almonds. Return to oven for 10 minutes. Cool on a rack.

© Williams-Sonoma

Sweet Snack Mix

6 *cups crunchy sweetened corn and oat cereal or sweetened wheat puffs*
1½ *cups miniature marshmallows*
1½ *cups semi-sweet chocolate chips*
¼ *cup salted peanuts*

Combine all ingredients in a bowl and toss lightly to mix. Serve as a snack. Makes about 8 cups.

Thanks to General Foods

Polka Dot Peanut Butter Jumbos

1 cup margarine
1 cup peanut butter
1 cup granulated sugar
1 cup brown sugar, firmly packed
2 eggs
2 cups flour
1 teaspoon baking soda
1½ cups M&M's Plain or Peanut Chocolate Candies

Oven temperature: 350°F

Beat together margarine, peanut butter and sugars until light and fluffy; blend in eggs. Add combined flour and soda; mix well. Stir in M&M candies. Drop dough by level ¼ cup measures onto greased cookie sheets, about 3 inches apart. Bake 12-15 minutes or until edges are golden brown. Cool on cookie sheet for 3 minutes; remove to wire rack to cool thoroughly. Makes 2 dozen 4-inch cookies.

Thanks to M&M Candies

Sutter's Gold Chocolate Chip Cookies

1 cup butter or margarine, softened
½ cup granulated sugar
½ cup brown sugar, firmly packed
2 eggs
2 tablespoons milk
1 teaspoon vanilla extract
2 cups flour
1 teaspoon baking powder
½ teaspoon baking soda
½ teaspoon salt
12 ounces Ghirardelli Semi-sweet
    Chocolate Chips
3 cups wheat cereal flakes
Cinnamon sugar

Oven temperature: 350°F

Cream butter with sugar, brown sugar, eggs, milk and vanilla. Combine flour with baking powder, baking soda, salt; blend into creamed mixture. Stir in chocolate chips and cereal. Drop by teaspoon onto greased baking sheet. Sprinkle with cinnamon sugar. Bake 10 minutes. Makes 6 dozen cookies.

Baker Beach Picnic Cookies: Follow above recipe, substituting 2 cups crushed potato chips for wheat cereal flakes. Bake as directed.

Thanks to Ghirardelli Chocolate Company

Peanut Butter Chocolate Chip Cookies

½ cup peanut butter
½ cup butter or margarine, softened
½ cup packed brown sugar
¼ cup granulated sugar
1 teaspoon vanilla extract
1 egg
1 tablespoon water
1 cup flour
½ teaspoon salt
½ teaspoon baking powder
¾ cup chopped peanuts
6 ounces Ghirardelli Semi-sweet Chocolate Chips

Oven temperature: 350°F

Cream peanut butter with butter, adding brown sugar, sugar, vanilla, egg and water. Combine flour with salt and baking powder. Gradually add dry ingredients to creamed mixture. Stir in peanuts and chocolate chips. Drop by teaspoon onto ungreased baking sheets. To flatten cookies, crisscross with fork. Bake 10-12 minutes. Makes 5 dozen cookies.

Thanks to Ghirardelli Chocolate Company

Cocoa Kiss Cookies

1 cup butter or margarine
⅔ cup granulated sugar
1 teaspoon vanilla extract
1⅔ cups unsifted all-purpose flour
¼ cup Hershey's Cocoa
1 cup finely chopped pecans
1 9-ounce package (about 54)
   Hershey's Kisses, unwrapped
Confectioners' sugar

Oven temperature: 375°F

Cream butter or margarine, sugar and vanilla in large mixer bowl. Combine flour and cocoa; blend into creamed mixture. Add nuts; beat on low speed until well blended. Chill dough about 1 hour or until firm enough to handle. Shape scant tablespoon of dough around Kiss, covering completely. Shape into balls; place on ungreased cookie sheet. Bake at 375°F for 10-12 minutes or until set. Cool slightly; remove to wire rack and cool completely. Roll in confectioners' sugar. Roll in additional confectioners' sugar just before serving. Makes about 4½ dozen 1-inch cookies.

Thanks to Hershey Foods Corporation

Three Layer Ghirardelli Squares

1½ cups graham cracker crumbs
¼ cup brown sugar
6 tablespoons butter or margarine, melted
Pinch nutmeg
12 ounces Ghirardelli Semi-sweet Chocolate Chips
1 cup flaked coconut
1 cup chopped pecans or walnuts
1 jar (7 ounces) marshmallow creme
2 tablespoons milk
1 teaspoon vanilla extract

Oven temperature: 350°F

Combine graham cracker crumbs, sugar and butter. Press into a 9" x 13" pan. Bake for 10 minutes; remove from oven. Mix chocolate chips with coconut and nuts. Spread over first layer. Thin marshmallow creme with milk and vanilla. Drizzle over top. Bake an additional 15 minutes. Cool before cutting into squares. Makes 32 pieces.

Thanks to Ghirardelli Chocolate Company

Granny's Healthy Cookies

½ cup sweet butter
½ cup granulated sugar
½ cup brown sugar, *firmly packed*
1 egg
1 teaspoon vanilla extract
1 tablespoon milk
1½ cups flour
1 teaspoon baking soda
½ teaspoon salt
1 teaspoon cinnamon
1 teaspoon nutmeg
½ cup oats
½ cup toasted wheat germ
½ cup raisins
6 ounces semi-sweet chocolate chips

Oven temperature: 375°F

Beat together butter and sugars, then add egg, vanilla, milk. Sift together flour, baking soda, salt, cinnamon, nutmeg and beat into liquid mixture. Fold in oats, wheat germ, raisins and chocolate chips. Drop by teaspoon onto greased cookie sheets. Bake 10-12 minutes or until golden brown. Makes 4 dozen cookies.

Oatmeal Chocolate Chip Walnut Cookies

Beat together:
- 1 cup brown sugar
- 1 cup white sugar
- 1 cup softened butter

Add:
- 2 teaspoons vanilla extract
- 2 tablespoons milk
- 2 lightly beaten eggs

Sift together and stir:
- 2 cups flour
- 1 teaspoon salt
- 1 teaspoon baking soda
- 1 teaspoon baking powder

Stir in by hand:
- 2½ cups old-fashioned oats
- 12 ounces chocolate chips
- 1½ cups chopped walnuts

Drop onto a greased cookie sheet. Bake at 350°F for 12-15 minutes. For a fatter cookie, chill the dough before baking, then roll into small balls and place on the greased cookie sheet. Makes about 4 dozen cookies.

Thanks to The Commissary, Philadelphia, Pa.

Everything But The Kitchen Sink Cookies

¾ cup butter or margarine
½ cup granulated sugar
½ cup brown sugar
1 egg
1 teaspoon vanilla
1½ cups flour
½ teaspoon baking soda
½ teaspoon salt
1 teaspoon cinnamon
1 cup mashed banana
1½ cups oats
½ cup raisins
1 cup semi-sweet chocolate chips

Oven temperature: 375°F

Cream together butter and sugars until light and fluffy. Beat in egg and vanilla. Sift together and add flour, baking soda, salt and cinnamon; blend well. Fold in banana, oats, raisins and chocolate chips. Drop by teaspoon onto greased cookie sheets. Bake 10-12 minutes or until golden. Makes 4 dozen cookies.

Marshmallow-Topped Triple Chocolate Cake

1 *package (2-layer size) chocolate cake mix or pudding-included cake mix*
1 *package (4-serving size) chocolate flavor instant pudding and pie filling*
1¾ *cups milk*
2 *eggs*
12 *ounces semi-sweet chocolate chips*
1 *cup chocolate syrup*
3 *cups miniature marshmallows*

Oven temperature: 350°F

Combine cake mix, pudding mix, milk, eggs and chocolate chips in a large bowl. Mix by hand until blended, about 2 minutes. Pour into a greased and floured 13" x 9" pan and bake 50-55 minutes or until cake springs back when lightly pressed. Drizzle ½ cup of the chocolate syrup over warm cake and sprinkle with marshmallows. Bake about 5 minutes longer or until marshmallows are softened and lightly browned. Drizzle with remaining syrup. Cool in pan and cut into squares using a knife dipped in warm water.

In high-altitude areas: Use large eggs, add ⅓ cup all-purpose flour and 1¼ cups water; reduce milk to ½ cup. Bake at 375°F for 50 minutes. (With pudding-included cake mix, add 1 cup water.)

Thanks to General Foods

Fortified & Pasteurized Cookies

2½ cups flour
1 teaspoon salt
1 teaspoon baking soda
1 cup butter
1 cup granulated sugar
1 cup brown sugar, firmly packed
2 eggs
⅓ cup buttermilk
1 teaspoon vanilla extract
12 ounces semi-sweet chocolate chips
1 cup raisins

Oven temperature: 375°F

Sift together flour, salt and baking soda. In a separate bowl cream together butter and sugars. Beat in eggs, one at a time, then buttermilk and vanilla. Combine flour mixture with liquid mixture; blend well. Fold in chocolate chips and raisins. Drop by teaspoonful onto greased cookie sheets. Bake 10-12 minutes. Makes 5 dozen cookies.

Double Chocolate Chip Cookies

½ cup butter or margarine
1 cup brown sugar, firmly packed
1 egg
½ cup sour cream
1 teaspoon vanilla extract
12 ounces Ghirardelli Semi-sweet Chocolate Chips
1¾ cups unsifted flour
½ teaspoon salt
½ teaspoon baking powder
½ teaspoon baking soda
½ cup chopped pecans
¼ cup chopped maraschino cherries (optional)

Oven temperature: 350°F

Cream butter with brown sugar. Mix in egg, sour cream, vanilla. Melt 6 ounces chocolate chips and blend with creamed mixture. Mix flour with salt, baking powder and baking soda. Add dry ingredients to creamed mixture, stirring until smooth. Fold in nuts, well-drained cherries and remaining chocolate chips. Drop by heaping teaspoon onto greased baking sheet. Bake 10-12 minutes or until slightly cracked on top. Makes 5 dozen cookies.

Thanks to Ghirardelli Chocolate Company

Would You Believe Banana & Oats Cookies?

½ cup butter or margarine
½ cup granulated sugar
½ cup brown sugar
1 egg
1 teaspoon vanilla extract
1¼ cups flour
½ teaspoon baking soda
½ teaspoon salt
1½ cups oats
1 cup mashed banana
6 ounces chocolate chips

Oven temperature: 375°F

Combine butter with sugars and beat until fluffy. Beat in egg and vanilla. Sift together and combine flour, baking soda and salt; blend well. Fold in oats, banana and chocolate chips. Drop by teaspoon onto greased cookie sheets. Bake 10 minutes or until golden brown. Makes 4½ dozen cookies.

Snap, Crackle, Pop & Oats

2 cups flour
1 teaspoon baking soda
½ teaspoon baking powder
½ teaspoon salt
1 cup butter or margarine
¾ cup granulated sugar
¾ cup brown sugar, firmly packed
2 eggs
1 teaspoon vanilla extract
¾ cup oats
6 ounces chocolate chips
1 cup walnuts
1 cup toasted crisp rice cereal

Oven temperature: 350°F

In a large bowl, sift flour, baking soda, baking powder and salt. In a separate bowl, cream together butter and sugars. Add eggs and vanilla; beat well. Stir dry ingredients into mixture. Fold in oats, chocolate chips, walnuts and cereal. Drop by teaspoonful onto greased cookie sheets. Bake 10-12 minutes. Makes 5 dozen cookies.

Puckered Cookies

½ cup butter or margarine
⅓ cup granulated sugar
⅔ cup brown sugar, firmly packed
1 teaspoon vanilla extract
1 egg
1 tablespoon grated lemon rind
1 tablespoon lemon juice
1¼ cups sifted flour
½ teaspoon baking soda
½ teaspoon salt
½ cup oats
6 ounces semi-sweet chocolate chips

Oven temperature: 375°F

Cream together butter and sugars until light and fluffy. Add egg, lemon rind and lemon juice and beat well. Sift together and add flour, baking soda and salt. Fold in oats and chocolate chips. Drop by teaspoon onto greased cookie sheets. Bake 10-12 minutes or until golden brown. Makes 4 dozen cookies.

Guittard Milk Chocolate Fudge Candy

Melt in top of double boiler over hot tap water one 12-ounce package Guittard Milk Chocolate Chips. Stir in ¼ cup (2 ounces) evaporated milk, ⅛ teaspoon salt, ½ teaspoon vanilla. Mix well until smooth. Add to mixture ½ cup chopped nuts. Pour into lightly greased 8-inch pan and cool. Cut into squares. Makes about 1½ cups fudge or approximately 1 pound.

Thanks to Guittard Chocolate Company

Reese's Cookies

1 cup shortening or ¾ cup butter or margarine, softened
1 cup granulated sugar
½ cup brown sugar, packed
1 teaspoon vanilla extract
2 eggs
2 cups unsifted all-purpose flour
1 teaspoon baking soda
1 cup Reese's Peanut Butter Flavored Chips
1 cup Hershey's Semi-Sweet Chocolate Chips

Oven temperature: 350°F

Cream shortening or butter or margarine, granulated sugar, brown sugar and vanilla until light and fluffy. Add eggs and beat well. Combine flour and baking soda; add to creamed mixture. Stir in peanut butter chips and chocolate chips. Drop by teaspoonful onto ungreased cookie sheet. Bake at 350°F for 10-12 minutes or until lightly browned. Cool slightly; remove to wire rack and cool completely. Makes about 5 dozen 2½-inch cookies.

1982 © Hershey Foods Corporation

George Washington's Favorites

2¼ cups unsifted flour
½ teaspoon salt
1 teaspoon baking soda
1 cup butter or margarine
¾ cup granulated sugar
¾ cup brown sugar, firmly packed
2 eggs
1 teaspoon vanilla extract
12 ounces semi-sweet chocolate chips
1 cup chopped walnuts
½ cup red maraschino cherries,
    drained and chopped

Oven temperature: 375°F

Sift together flour, salt and baking soda. In a separate bowl, cream together butter and sugars. Add eggs and vanilla and beat well. Stir flour mixture into liquid mixture. Fold in chocolate chips, nuts and cherries. Drop by teaspoonful onto ungreased cookie sheets. Bake 10-12 minutes. Makes 5 dozen cookies.

Vitamin C Cookies

½ cup butter or margarine
½ cup granulated sugar
½ cup dark brown sugar
1 egg
1 teaspoon vanilla extract
1 tablespoon orange juice
½ tablespoon grated orange rind
¾ cup flour
½ teaspoon baking soda
½ teaspoon salt
1½ cups oats
6 ounces chocolate chips

Oven temperature: 375°F

Cream butter and sugars until fluffy. Beat in egg, vanilla, orange juice and orange rind. Sift together and add flour, baking soda, salt. Fold in oats and chocolate chips, blending all ingredients well. Drop by teaspoon onto greased cookie sheets. Bake 10-12 minutes or until lightly browned.

Colorful Chocolate Chippers

¾ cup butter or margarine
1⅓ cups firmly packed light brown
  sugar
2 eggs
1 teaspoon vanilla extract
2¼ cups flour
1 teaspoon baking soda
½ teaspoon salt
1 cup M&M's Plain Chocolate
  Candies
½ cup chopped nuts

Oven temperature: 350°F

Beat together butter and sugar until light and fluffy; blend in eggs and vanilla. Add sifted flour, soda and salt; mix well. Stir in M&M's and nuts. Drop dough by heaping tablespoonful onto greased cookie sheets about 3 inches apart. Bake 9-10 minutes or until lightly browned. Cool on cookie sheet about 3 minutes; remove cookies to wire rack to cool thoroughly. Makes 2 dozen 3½-inch cookies.

Thanks to M&M Candies

Redwood Camp Squares

½ cup butter or margarine
¼ cup sugar
½ cup brown sugar, firmly packed
2 eggs, beaten
1½ teaspoons vanilla extract
½ cup rolled oats
1 cup flour
½ teaspoon baking soda
¼ teaspoon salt
⅛ teaspoon cinnamon
½ cup chopped peanuts
6 ounces Ghirardelli Semi-sweet
    Chocolate Chips

Oven temperature: 350°F

Lightly cream butter and sugars. Add eggs and vanilla. (Mixture will be lumpy.) Stir in oats. Sift flour with baking soda, salt, cinnamon. Mix dry ingredients into creamed mixture. Fold in peanuts and chocolate chips. Spread dough into greased 9″ x 13″ baking pan. Bake 20 minutes. Cool before cutting into squares. Makes 24 2-inch squares.

Thanks to Ghirardelli Chocolate Company

Crazy Microwave Cookies

¼ cup butter or margarine
¾ cup graham cracker crumbs
½ cup peanut butter chips
½ cup chocolate chips
1 cup shredded coconut
½ cup chopped nuts
1 can (14 ounces) sweetened condensed milk

Microwave power level: High (100%) and Medium (50%)

Place butter in an 8" x 8" x 2" baking dish. Microwave on High (100%) for 45 seconds-1 minute or until melted. Stir in graham cracker crumbs until well blended. Press evenly in bottom of dish. Microwave on High (100%) for 2-3 minutes or until set; turn baking dish a half-turn halfway through cooking. Layer each of the remaining ingredients in the order listed. Microwave on Medium (50%) for 6-8 minutes or until bubbly. Allow to stand on a solid surface until completely cooled. Cut into bars. Makes 1 dozen bars.

© The Tappan Company — 1979

Peanut Blossoms

½ cup shortening
¾ cup peanut butter
⅓ cup granulated sugar
⅓ cup brown sugar, packed
1 egg
2 tablespoons milk
1 teaspoon vanilla extract
1⅓ cups unsifted all-purpose flour
1 teaspoon baking soda
½ teaspoon salt
Granulated sugar
1 9-ounce package (about 54)
   Hershey's Kisses, unwrapped

Oven temperature: 375°F

Cream shortening and peanut butter; add granulated sugar and brown sugar. Add egg, milk and vanilla; beat well. Combine flour, baking soda and salt; gradually add to creamed mixture, blending thoroughly. Shape dough into 1-inch balls; roll in granulated sugar. Place on ungreased cookie sheet; bake at 375°F for 10-12 minutes. Remove from oven; immediately place Kiss on top of each cookie, pressing down so that cookie cracks around edge. Remove to wire rack and cool completely. Makes about 4 dozen 1½-inch cookies.

Thanks to Hershey Foods Corporation

Merle's Chocolate Chip Peach Loaf

Oven temperature: 350°F

Sift together:
  2 cups flour
  1 teaspoon baking soda
  ¼ teaspoon salt
  1½ teaspoons cinnamon
  ½ teaspoon nutmeg
  ½ teaspoon mace
Work in with a fork or fingertips:
  ½ cup butter or margarine
Add: 1 cup granulated sugar

In a blender mix until smooth:
  2 cups peeled, sliced fresh peaches
  1 egg
  ¼ cup buttermilk
  2 tablespoons molasses

Add to flour-margarine-sugar mixture; blend well. Fold in one 6-ounce package semi-sweet chocolate chips. Pour mixture into a greased loaf pan. Bake 1 hour or until an inserted toothpick comes out clean.

Note: You also may bake this cake in an 8-inch square pan. Bake at 350°F for 30-40 minutes.

Toll House® Pie

2 eggs
½ cup unsifted flour
½ cup granulated sugar
½ cup brown sugar, firmly packed
1 cup butter, melted and cooled to room temperature
1 6-ounce package Nestlé's Semi-Sweet Real Chocolate Morsels
1 cup chopped walnuts
1 9-inch unbaked pie shell
Whipped cream or ice cream (optional)

Oven temperature: 325°F

In a large bowl, beat eggs until foamy; beat in flour, sugar and brown sugar until well blended. Blend in melted butter. Stir in Nestlé's Semi-Sweet Real Chocolate Morsels and walnuts. Pour into pie shell. Bake 1 hour. Remove from oven and serve with whipped cream or ice cream. Makes one 9-inch pie.

© The Nestlé Company

Everything On The Spice Rack Cookies

2½ cups flour
½ teaspoon salt
1 teaspoon baking soda
1 teaspoon cinnamon
½ teaspoon cloves
½ teaspoon ginger
½ teaspoon nutmeg
½ cup butter or margarine
1 cup granulated sugar
1 cup brown sugar, firmly packed
2 eggs, beaten
1 teaspoon vanilla extract
⅔ cup sour cream
12 ounces semi-sweet chocolate chips
1 cup chopped walnuts

Oven temperature: 350°F

Sift together flour, salt, baking soda and spices. In a separate bowl, cream together butter and sugars. Add eggs and vanilla; mix well. Add dry ingredients and sour cream until all ingredients are blended together. Fold in chocolate chips and walnuts. Drop from a teaspoon onto greased cookie sheets. Bake 10-12 minutes or until golden brown. Makes 5 dozen cookies.

Not Bad Cookies, Actually

½ cup butter or margarine
½ cup granulated sugar
1 cup brown sugar, firmly packed
1 egg, lightly beaten
⅓ cup milk
1 teaspoon vanilla extract
1 cup sifted flour
½ teaspoon salt
½ teaspoon baking soda
½ teaspoon cinnamon
2½ cups oats
1 cup chopped walnuts
6 ounces semi-sweet chocolate chips

Oven temperature: 350°F

Cream together butter and sugars. Beat in egg, milk and vanilla. In a separate bowl, mix flour, salt, baking soda, cinnamon, then combine with liquid mixture. Fold in oats, walnuts and chocolate chips. Place approximately 2 cups of batter on each of 2 foil-lined and greased 12-inch pizza pans. Spread dough to within a 1-inch distance of the pans' rims. Bake 15 minutes or until golden brown. Cool. Cut into pizzalike wedges to serve. Makes 2 giant cookies.

Mousse au Chocolat

1 9-inch graham cracker crust
6 ounces semi-sweet chocolate
  morsels
6 eggs
1 teaspoon instant coffee
1 cup granulated sugar

Melt chocolate chips on top of double boiler over medium flame. Separate eggs. Keep 5-6 whites and 3 yolks. Beat egg whites constantly for 5 minutes using electric mixer. Remove all lumps. Peaks must be very white and stiff. Beat egg yolks with a fork till foamy. Pour into melted chocolate and mix well. Make 1 cup of instant coffee. Place 3 teaspoons into chocolate-egg yolk mixture. Gradually beat 1 cup sugar into whites. Peaks will be slightly less stiff. Fold egg white mixture into chocolate mixture, using a wooden spoon. Blend well. Pour mixture into graham cracker crust. Refrigerate at least 2 hours. Garnish with whipped cream if desired before serving.

Thanks, Sandy

Flap Jack Cookies

½ cup butter or margarine, softened
½ cup dark brown sugar, firmly
    packed
⅓ cup granulated sugar
1 egg
1 teaspoon vanilla extract
1 cup flour
½ teaspoon baking powder
½ teaspoon salt
¼ teaspoon cinnamon
¾ cup quick rolled oats
6 ounces Ghirardelli Semi-sweet
    Chocolate Chips

Oven temperature: 375°F

Cream butter lightly with sugars. Blend in egg and vanilla. Sift flour with baking powder, salt, cinnamon. Stir in dry ingredients, rolled oats, chocolate chips. Do not overmix. Use ice cream scoop to drop cookies onto greased baking sheets. Flatten with pancake turner dipped lightly in flour. Bake 10-12 minutes. Makes 12 4-inch cookies.

Thanks to Ghirardelli Chocolate Company

Gingerbread Square Things That Are Not Cookies

2 eggs, *lightly beaten*
1 cup sour cream
½ cup molasses
½ cup brown sugar
1½ cups flour
½ teaspoon salt
1 teaspoon baking soda
1½ teaspoons ginger
1 teaspoon cinnamon
½ cup melted butter or margarine
6 ounces semi-sweet chocolate chips
1 cup chopped walnuts

Oven temperature: 350°F

Combine eggs, sour cream, molasses and brown sugar; beat well. Sift together and add flour, salt, baking soda, ginger and cinnamon. Add butter and blend well. Fold in chocolate chips and walnuts. Pour into greased 8-inch baking pan. Bake for 30 minutes. Cool and cut into squares. Top with whipped cream.

Guittard Milk Chocolate Chip Cookies

Preheat oven to 375°F

Cream together
  ¾ cup butter or margarine
  ¾ cup granulated sugar
  1 teaspoon vanilla extract
  ¼ cup brown sugar, firmly
    packed
Beat and add
  1 egg
Sift together and add
  1⅔ cups sifted flour
  ¾ teaspoon salt
  ½ teaspoon baking soda

Mix well. If batter is too stiff, add 1-2 teaspoons water. Stir in one 12-ounce package Guittard Milk Chocolate Chips. Drop batter by well-rounded half-teaspoons onto greased cookie sheets. Bake 10-12 minutes. Makes 60-70 cookies.

Thanks to Guittard Chocolate Company

Aunt Bernice's Chocolate Cake

1 *package yellow cake mix*
1 *package instant chocolate pudding*
1 *cup sour cream*
4 *eggs*
½ *cup oil*
1 *teaspoon vanilla*
1 *cup chopped walnuts*
1 *cup semi-sweet chocolate chips*
3 *tablespoons rum*

Oven temperature: 325°F

Mix all ingredients except nuts and chocolate chips by hand for about 7 minutes. Should be very well blended. Fold in nuts and chocolate chips. Pour into a greased and lightly floured 10-inch bundt pan. Bake 1 hour. Cool. If desired, frost or sprinkle with confectioners' sugar.

You also can make a layer cake by baking in two 9-inch layer pans. The cake is so rich that it really doesn't need frosting.

Special thanks to Elizabeth J. Sussman

Chocolate Chip Cream Cheese Cookies

1 cup butter
1 cup granulated sugar
1 3-ounce package cream cheese
2 eggs
2 tablespoons grated orange rind
2 teaspoons vanilla extract
2 cups sifted flour
1 teaspoon salt
12 ounces chocolate chips

Oven temperature: 350°F

Cream together butter, sugar and cream cheese thoroughly. Add eggs, orange rind and vanilla, beat well. Stir in flour and salt. Fold in chocolate chips. Bake on greased cookie sheets 12-15 minutes. Makes 5 dozen cookies.

Chocolate Chip Pancakes or Waffles

1 cup pancake mix
¼ cup semi-sweet chocolate chips

Prepare pancake mix as directed on package, adding the chocolate chips before cooking as pancakes or waffles. Serve as a dessert topped with powdered sugar, syrup or a sauce, if desired. Makes six pancakes or waffles.

Thanks to General Foods

Haight-Ashbury Granola Cookies

1 cup regular rolled oats
2 tablespoons oil
½ cup butter or margarine, softened
½ cup honey
½ cup brown sugar, firmly packed
1 egg
¼ cup wheat germ
1 teaspoon vanilla extract
1½ teaspoons cinnamon
¼ teaspoon allspice
1½ cups unbleached flour
¾ teaspoon salt
½ teaspoon baking powder
½ teaspoon baking soda
¼ cup milk
¾ cup chopped dates
¾ cup chopped walnuts
¾ cup flaked coconut
6 ounces Ghirardelli Semi-sweet
   Chocolate Chips

Oven temperature: 350°F

In baking pan, toss oats with oil. Toast oats in oven at 350°F for 15 minutes, stirring once. Cream butter with honey, brown sugar, egg, vanilla and spices. Mix in wheat germ. Mix flour with salt, baking powder, baking soda. Mix dry ingredients into creamed mixture, alternating with milk. Stir in toasted oats, dates, nuts, coconut, chocolate chips. Drop by teaspoon onto greased baking sheet. Bake at 350°F for 9-10 minutes. Makes 7 dozen cookies.

Thanks to Ghirardelli Chocolate Company

Golden Nugget Cookies

¾ cup butter or margarine
1 cup sugar
1 egg
½ teaspoon vanilla extract
½ teaspoon cinnamon
½ teaspoon nutmeg
1 cup mashed, ripe bananas
1½ cups flour
½ teaspoon salt
½ teaspoon baking soda
1 cup rolled oats
6 ounces Ghirardelli Semi-sweet
  Chocolate Chips

Oven temperature: 375°F

Cream together butter, sugar, egg, vanilla, cinnamon, nutmeg. Beat in bananas. Combine flour, salt, baking soda; stir into creamed mixture. Fold in oats and chocolate chips. Drop by teaspoon onto greased baking sheet. Bake 8 minutes. Makes 3 dozen cookies.

Thanks to Ghirardelli Chocolate Company